SPIRITUAL
SENSES

D1219748

SPIRITUAL SENSES

T. Austin-Sparks

LIFE SENTENCE Publishing, LLC

Spiritual Senses

RELIGION / Christianity / General

ISBN 13: 978-0-9832016-6-3

Available from the Publishers at:

(at the price of your choice)
www.lifesentencepublishing.com
715.223.3013

Also available from:
Amazon.com
Barnesandnoble.com
And more...

Printed in the United States of America

Contents

Publisher's Note

With the exception of minor corrections, all of this book's content remains unchanged from the original words of T. Austin-Sparks, taken from the website of www.austin-sparks.net. In keeping with T. Austin-Sparks' wishes, this book is available for free at www.lifesentencepublishing.com. Please continue to respect T. Austin-Sparks' wishes in that what was freely received should be freely given. We ask, as is asked on the website, that if you choose to share this book with others, that you please respect his wishes and offer it freely – free of changes, free of charge, and free of copyright. It is our pleasure to bring glory to God's Kingdom by making this book available to those who may otherwise not have received some of the wisdom of Christ through the pen of T. Austin-Sparks.

Jeremiah M. Zeiset
LIFE SENTENCE Publishing, LLC
Wisconsin, US, 2011

Part I

The Spiritual Clinic

Chapter 1

Paralysis

The Paralysis of Disappointed Expectations

There are not a few typical instances of such in the Word of God. Some of these are discerned in ejaculatory and fragmentary expressions, such as that of Job, "My purposes are broken off"; or of the two on the Emmaus Road - "But we trusted..." or, again, of John the Baptist - "Art thou he that cometh, or look we for another?"

And then as to the man who has come to be known as "The Rich Fool," there are two fragments in the narrative - "He said... but God said."

In each case there was an arriving at an end, a deadlock, a paralysis, and each represented a false expectation.

Two of these at least (i.e. John the Baptist and the Emmaus Road) were to be accounted for by a mistaken conception. This conception is very far reaching today and has become responsible for much deception; a deception which works in two ways. On the one hand many give up in despair - like John the Baptist - because the issues which they had come to believe were immediately inseparable from a certain acceptance and line of action have not developed; the results have not followed, the success has not materialized. On the other hand, many have been ensnared by this false conception into thinking that a certain kind of success, increase, popularity, achievement, is THE thing, while - as a matter of fact - the ultimate spiritual value is almost if not entirely lacking.

In these two cases there were at least two further fundamental misconceptions which issued in paralysis. One was the failure to recognize the initial, primary, and essentially spiritual nature of Christ's mission and work. In their minds the temporal and earthly bulked upon the horizon to the exclusion of the spiritual and heavenly. We think it unnecessary for us to show how much this was so. It is one of the most obvious things in the Gospels, and was one of the Master's greatest problems with His disciples. Again and again, He tried to let in light to correct this misconception, and knew that it would be the ground upon which at last they would all be offended, the difficulty over which they would all stumble, when they saw Him an apparently helpless victim on the Cross.

There was also a total misconception of the order of events, as Acts 15:14-16 (R.V.) clearly shows. There was a complete incapacity to recognize the Divine purpose, method, means, time, instrument, basis, and passion. This let in personal interests, concerns, ambitions, and false anxieties. The thwarting of these, and the disillusionment of the Cross smashed them and their whole scheme of things.

"But we trusted," said they; but their thought was earthbound. Something of "the heavenly vision" is essential to life and assurance and hope and ascendancy. We shall find increasingly that before there can be an earth-and-world-manifestation of the sovereignty of Christ in anything like a commensurate sense, there will be an intense heavenliness and spirituality of life and work on the part of those who are called to share the Throne.

Whatever else may have been in John's mind leading to his pathetic and despairing message, it is almost certain that his own condition presented a problem occasioned by a mistaken idea. It would be something like this: 'If He really is the Christ, and all that has been prophesied of Him is true - all those things about opening the prisons to the prisoners, and letting the oppressed go free, etc. - why is it that I, having served Him as I have and standing in such a relationship to Him as I do, should be left in this dungeon? There are reports of miracles and mighty works. Why am I left to suffer thus?' This problem comes near to the heart of many of the Lord's people. We know from the Master Himself that He was far from ignoring or forgetting John. In John's case it is certain that not for sin or in Divine forgetfulness was he left in his trial undelivered. The reason was to be found elsewhere.

It might be as well to listen to another who has a different expectation without despair: "The Holy Ghost witnesseth in every city, saying that bonds and afflictions abide me." This one had much to say about the spiritual fruitfulness of his bonds.

"I am an ambassador in bonds for the mystery of the Gospel."

"My bonds *in Christ* are manifest in all the palace and in all other places."

"Many of the brethren, waxing confident by my bonds, are much more bold to speak the word."

"Whom I have begotten in my bonds."

It may hardly seem fair to make this comparison between the two men, but one does it only because one finds so many where John was; and who is to know but that Paul sometimes was tempted to feel that way? The facts are that there is often a larger service through a certain curtailment, a fuller life through a deeper death, a richer gain by a keener loss; and we have to look for the impact of the operation of God in us in a realm where the eye of man cannot trace. The Master said of John that he was the greatest of the prophets; and he, no less than they, was to lay down his life and suffer unto death for his testimony. There is evidently in the eyes of God a virtue in certain sufferings of His servants which is of greater importance to Him than the fleeting glory which might accrue to Him by His deliverance of them. There is that peculiar blessedness, to which the Lord referred in His reply to John, which belongs to them who under severe trial are "not offended in Him." In some strange way John was related to the Cross and to "the Lamb of God," and thus he was brought within the realm of "the offence of the Cross."

What do we expect in our relationship to "the testimony of Jesus"? Supposing the deepest purposes of God can only be realized by His hiding from our flesh all that our flesh craves for in its life, and - more - supposing His work in us, whereby triumphant faith and obedience reach their highest form, necessitates His concealing Himself and accepting the risk of being considered to have been unfaithful? There is no doubt that most of those who have been called into some of the most vital expressions of "the eternal purpose" have been trained in the school of *apparent* Divine contradiction, delay, withdrawal, and darkness. Paul wrote to the Thessalonian saints that "no man should be moved by these afflictions for... we are *appointed* thereunto."

Job, who cried "My purposes are broken off," learned that that did not matter very much seeing that God's greater purposes stood fast. It all depends upon whether we know that we are in "His purpose" and in His way of fulfillment, whether in the day of the ordeal we shall triumph or be paralyzed.

Job found strength in recognizing that "He performeth the thing that is appointed for me, and many such things are with him," in spite of those things being quite foreign to his own expectation.

A right and true relationship to the Lord is a basis upon which there is absolute confidence, assurance, and hope when our purposes or expectations are shattered. It was not so in the case of the "rich fool." "He said..." He had purposes of his own unrelated to God. "But God said..." and that was the end of all purpose.

If we have God's life in us we can survive anything. The Lord is not out to peevishly frustrate our hopes or disappoint our expectations, but to either change them for His own or fulfill them in a higher and larger realm.

May we just add a word in this general connection? Many unexpected things, and things quite contrary to expectation, will come to us in the realms of both spiritual experience and Christian service, but one of the bitterest and often most fatal forms of this paralysis comes through disappointed expectations with regard to people. David said *in his haste* "all men are a lie"; and many others have come perilously near to feeling that they dare not put any confidence in anyone. David's experience of the breakdown and worse of the familiar friend who went to the house of God with him has been that of many others. Trusted and highly esteemed leaders, conspicuous and greatly used men of God, such as we had come to trust and look up to and count upon and regard as authorities or counselors, saints and deeply taught: these all in one or more of many ways may cause us to reel under the shock of a disillusionment - a manifestation of ill-temper, irritability, jealousy, personal interest, pride, respect of persons, suspicion; concern for place, prestige, approval; being influenced by hearsay, report, criticism; prejudice, partiality, compromise: all these or others, and some very much worse. Anyone who reads this will understand what is meant and will be well able to appreciate the acute suffering and resultant numbness and paralysis of such an experience as it strikes at the vitals of faith, fellowship and trust. There are so many embittered and skeptical, soured and suspicious, because of such disappointed expectations, and too often they allow it to strike at their faith in God.

Now the first thing to say is that the Lord has prescribed very carefully for this form of paralysis, both for prevention and cure. He has pointed out the antidote both in word and deed. As to the word, at how much pains has God gone to warn against "putting trust in man." Again and again the danger and folly of making man a prop and a basis of confidence has been emphasized. As to the practical side, why - if not for this very purpose - has not the Lord prevented the disappointing and, sometimes, shameful breakdown of His best servants from being placed on record? If the Bible is inspired of God, then we have to place the record to the intention of God. It is strange that we so often extract the comfort for ourselves from this fact, but are shocked when we discover the "like passions" in certain others.

We had better settle it once and for all, be grateful as we should and must for all the grace of God in His children, value all the help through them, and esteem them very highly for their work's sake; the Lord will never allow us to go for long on human props or crutches, but will free us to see that He alone is our Rock, that our spiritual education and growth must ever and only rest upon *personal* and *direct* knowledge of Himself. The greater the usefulness to God of any life, the deeper the loneliness in experience. *He* takes us often where no others can enter, interpret, understand, help. Rather, by their mental play upon our strange experience, and their interpretations given to it, they create even greater painfulness and distress for us. Sooner or later we are bound to be disappointed in man but this may lead to a rich and deep knowledge of God if we are not soured and paralyzed by it.

It will also be the occasion of a great and healthy self-distrust on the one hand, and a deep sympathy and solicitude for the suffering on the other hand. The Master in the hour of anguish "looked for some to take pity, but there was none." We may be allowed just to sip the cup in order to know something of the help of God which no other can give.

Chapter 2

The Paralysis of a Spiritual Irregularity

From observation of the maladies which come upon the people of God and bring arrest to His work through them, we have been much impressed with the fact that the violation of a Divine order is the cause of much trouble. If it is true that what God is doing in this age is not just saving individuals as such but constituting a "Body" and building a "House" by the addition of each saved one, then the right position of each is vital to perfect functioning and heavenly order. There is an order, and there is a position for each member. It is not given to us - let us say it with emphasis - to appoint the place or to manipulate into position. That is the work of the Holy Spirit. What we do say is that each member has his or her place, and God knows what it is. Under the sovereignty of the Holy Spirit each member should come into that place. If they fail to do so, or get into a wrong place, they miss their essential ministry and upset the effectiveness of the Body.

"Now hath God set the members..." (1 Cor. 12:18).

"Unto each... was the grace given according to the measure of the gift of Christ" (Eph. 4:7).

"Having gifts differing according to the grace that was given to us..." (Rom. 12:6).

There are not a few illustrations of dislocation and irregularity in the Scriptures:

Dathan and Abiram and their company (Numbers 16).

Aaron and Miriam (Numbers 12).

Saul going over the head of Samuel (1 Sam. 13:9).

Uzziah presuming into the priest's office (2 Chron. 26:16).

Paul has very much to say on matters of order in the Church, and it is not merely the individual position which is of importance, but the relative factor and element. Independent action is as dangerous as dislocation - it robs of covering and protection and exposes to enemy forces. There is a heavenly order, a spiritual system, and the relationships and ministries of believers are to be according to those spiritual principles and a reflection of that heavenly order.

What Paul says about woman's place in ministry and the domestic relationships of the saints can only be understood and appreciated in this light.

When one called of God to do the work of an evangelist assumes the role of a teacher, or vice-versa, or any one marked out for a particular functioning attempts to do some other, or when one goes beyond the scope and assumes any prerogative which is not theirs by Divine ordering, they are in the way of an arrested ministry; and more, they will be landed into serious confusion. People and things - otherwise occupying a vital position in the Divine plan - put into their wrong places have the Divine unction withdrawn from them. This becomes manifest, and the spiritually undiscerning conclude that the thing or the person is outside the Divine purpose and accordingly rule them out. Thus much confusion and loss ensues.

Undoubtedly in New Testament times there was the recognition of the corporate nature of the Church, and the definite prayer, which followed the baptism of everyone who thereby testified to their identification with Christ, was the initial setting forth of this relative position and this truth of articulation, adjustment, and function. The Holy Ghost came in and took up the superintendence from that time, and any disorder thenceforth was against Him. In these few lines we have encircled a very wide and important field of truth and would plead for a prayerful retracing step by step with the Word.

The Holy Spirit's method is to set His seal upon us as we move according to His leading, not according to our fancy, choice, aptitude, predilection or ambition.

Chapter 3

Spiritual Neurasthenia

In the medical world this malady is described as "a condition of weakness and exhaustion of the nervous system, giving rise to various forms of mental and bodily inefficiency. The term covers an ill-defined, motley group of symptoms, which may be either general and the expression of derangement of the entire system, or local, limited to certain organs."

There is an almost appalling amount of this complaint about today, and a terrible prevalence amongst Christian workers. This is significant of a number of spiritual faults, to which we shall refer presently.

Before we deal with the spiritual side, it might be well and helpful if we said just a word about the natural in itself. This is one of those troubles so closely related to the mind that it forms peculiarly fruitful ground for the enemy.

For instance, apart from any spiritual factors, those who suffer from neurasthenia are subject to much depression, "low-spirits", and despondency; inability to perform the ordinary amount of mental work; loss of power of fixed attention so that, for example, a row of figures cannot be added up correctly, the dictating or writing of a few letters is a source of worry, petty details are a painful effort. Sleeplessness is often, but not always, a characteristic. Sometimes sensations of pain, usually localized, are present - a joint, a muscle, a sinew, a limb, the skin, the eyes, etc.; sometimes marked vertigo, almost like meningitis. Certain other peculiar symptoms of this malady are especially interesting as they come so near to what also characterizes supernatural or demoniacal cases.

For instance, in some cases there is a malicious delight in making people who are happier uncomfortable or miserable. Then a well-known symptom is the presence of a second something. When the mind is occupied - or straining to be occupied - with one thing, another thing or presence is shadowing the mental consciousness like a specter. Then again, the intrusion of uncontrollable thoughts foreign to the normal life, and often to the moral makeup, of the patient - cause intense distress. The desire to rush away and escape from everyone is very common, and also the tendency to fling oneself down in despair. Indeed, the symptoms are legion and vary with the degree and particular form of the complaint. We have only mentioned this much because it is possible to carry into the spiritual realm that which is not specifically spiritual, and relate either to the Lord, or to the enemy, that which may be simply infirmity of our body of corruption. At least it is as well that we recognize this, and know that our case is in common understanding amongst those who know; for a very general element of this trouble is that the patient always feels that he is completely misunderstood by all.

Confusion of Natural and Spiritual

When this distressing condition comes within the circle of God's people the enemy is especially active to give to it spiritual implications. What terrible distress there is abroad because of inability to concentrate the mind in prayer at once! What suffering because of depression which has been interpreted by the "accuser" as being the result of sin, thus setting up a false condemnation! What ravages by reason of that other presence being given a sinister character, as though the evil one had been given a right over one! What anguish because of those foreign thoughts! What lost assurance of salvation; sense of being beyond pardon; questioning the whole truth and reality of the Christian faith, etc., etc.!

Where shall we begin to help such afflicted ones?

First of all, let us say to all the Lord's people that we have one of the most serious warnings against living the Christian life in the realm of the soul instead of in the spirit. It would seem that the enemy would facilitate such "Christianity" to a tremendous degree. The mental, emotional, and volitional engrossment in "spiritual" things apart from or beyond a true Holy Spirit energizing will bring its own Nemesis, and the end may be despair.

"The mind of the flesh is death; but the mind of the spirit is life and peace."

Thus we would say that what is truly of the Spirit abides and stands when all the realm of the soul (psychical nature) and body breaks down and contradicts.

Have you been truly born from above? Have you been obedient to the heavenly vision, to the light, as you have had it? In failure and fall have you repentantly confessed, and done what could be done to bring forth fruit meet for repentance? Have you appealed to the efficacy of the Blood of Jesus Christ, God's Son? Have you kept short accounts with God when convicted of wrong? Then take your stand in your spirit, even against your own soul and body if needs be, and against all hell. Stand upon the fact that He in Whom you have put your trust is "greater than our heart."

Then, one word more. Keep your eyes outside. Refuse introspection, dwelling upon yourself, your condition, your feelings, your symptoms. Look not for hope in yourself. Seek no virtue in your own heart. Cease to expect any good of yourself, but remember that He is your righteousness, your surety, your acceptance with God, your merit, your Intercessor.

Chapter 4

Oneness with Christ and Mutual Relatedness

"For this cause many among you are weak and sickly, and not a few sleep" (1 Corinthians 11:30).

In the above words the Apostle gives the note he has made after holding a spiritual clinic in relation to the sicknesses and debilities among the Corinthian believers. Indeed, he goes beyond that and gives the reason for the death of "not a few." Evidently things were pretty bad, at that time, as to the physical. Incidentally, and yet as a striking part of the whole, it is impressive that so much physical sickness and - apparently - unnecessary death should be amongst those who were said to "come behind in no gift," including the gift of healing (1:7; 12:9).

Now let us clear this ground by saying emphatically that there was a definite reason for this condition, and evidently one which was based upon a state of things which should have been known to be wrong. That just means two things.

First, all sickness, ailment, and death is not due to specific sin on the part of the one afflicted. This surely goes without saying, but we say it strongly lest any sufferer should take on condemnation unnecessarily. There are many sufferers "in the will of God."

The other thing is that there must have been a knowledge which put these believers into the category of those who knew better and were not sinning in ignorance. It would indeed be a grievous thing if the Divine counsels decided that such a definite pronouncement should be made where people were totally ignorant of their sin and wrong doing.

The whole tone of this letter shows that the state of things was one which called for stern words and not soft advice.

That brings us right up to the very point of this particular word. There is a principle which we want to indicate. The actual nature of "not discerning the body" is not the object of our enquiry. The principle is this:-

If anyone or anybody of the Lord's people should have come to know of Divine truth, and should have definitely or ostensibly stood with it, they have come into touch, not with abstract doctrine, but with the Living God, and with that which involves Him. The effect must be either positively unto life or death. They can never remain as they were before; sooner or later there will be an issue. Should that Divine truth have come their way, or they have come its way, in something more than a mere tradition, that is, by a real first-hand work of the Holy Spirit, the issues will be the more immediate and positive. Should such a people - as in this basic instance at Corinth - know by a Holy Spirit ministry the truth of:

a) The essential vital oneness of believers with a crucified and risen Christ - implying their own death to the self-life, and resurrection to live "henceforth unto him" - and then bring their old nature life positively into the new realm, they must meet the impact of the death-dealing blow of the Cross.

Or should they know the truth of:

b) The essential oneness and relatedness of all believers as "one loaf, one body," and then act in any way which definitely violates that relatedness, such must suffer the consequences of getting away from the "covering" and safeguarding which - in some undefined, but very real way - is bound up with spiritual corporateness. There it is, and if we understood the laws and workings of the protective values of our physical bodies, and realized how a disturbed relatedness in function leads to suffering and death - unless put right - we should know that God has constituted the whole physical universe upon spiritual principles. Further, we should realize that the term "Body" as to the Church is no mere metaphor, but something very real.

It is just not possible to accept any Divine revelation without being involved in its principles, and suffering if those principles are violated. So the Apostle says "For this cause," i.e. the reason is this. You cannot profess that Christ is Lord, and then be your own Lord. You cannot be a member of a family and ignore the family and be as though you *were* the family. You cannot be a member of a body and then make your own plans and carry out your own arrangements without regard to laws of relatedness. This carries its own laws of retribution, but there is the Holy Spirit to be reckoned with and taken into account. We may slip up and the corrections of the Lord be gentle, but the matter of responsibility is one that varies according to opportunity, privilege, and position.

Part II

Spiritual Sight

Chapter 5

The Man Whose Eye is Opened

Then Jehovah opened the eyes of Balaam, and he saw the angel of Jehovah standing in the way (Num. 22:31).

Balaam the son of Beor saith, and the man whose eye is opened saith... falling down, and having his eyes open (Num. 24:3-4; A.R.V. Margin).

And they come to Jericho: and as He went out from Jericho, with His disciples and a great multitude, the son of Timaeus, Bartimaeus, a blind beggar, was sitting by the way side... And Jesus answered him, and said, "What wilt thou that I should do unto thee?" And the blind man said unto Him, "Rabboni, that I may receive my sight." And Jesus said unto him, "Go thy way; thy faith hath made thee whole." And straightway he received his sight, and followed Him in the way (Mark 10:46, 51-52).

And He took hold of the blind man by the hand, and brought him out of the village; and when He had spit on his eyes, and laid His hands upon him, He asked him, "Seest thou aught?" And he looked up, and said, "I see men; for behold them as trees, walking." Then again He laid His hands upon his eyes; and he looked stedfastly, and was restored, and saw all things clearly (Mark 8:23-25).

And as He passed by, He saw a man blind from his birth... and said unto him, "Go, wash in the pool of Siloam..." He went away therefore, and washed, and came seeing... He therefore answered,

"Whether he is a sinner, I know not: one thing I know, that, whereas I was blind, now I see (John 9:1, 7, 25).

...that the God of our Lord Jesus Christ, the Father of glory, may give unto you a spirit of wisdom and revelation in the knowledge of Him; having the eyes of your heart enlightened, that ye may know what is the hope of His calling, what the riches of the glory of His inheritance in the saints (Eph. 1:17-18).

I counsel thee to buy of Me gold refined by fire, that thou mayest become rich; and white garments, that thou mayest clothe thyself, and that the shame of thy nakedness be not made manifest; and eyesalve to anoint thine eyes, that thou mayest see (Rev. 3:18).

...to open their eyes, that they may turn from darkness to light and from the power of Satan unto God, that they may receive remission of sins and an inheritance among them that are sanctified by faith in Me (Acts 26:18).

I think the phrase used by Balaam might very well stand at the head of our present meditation - *"the man whose eye is opened"*.

The Root Malady of Our Time

As we contemplate the state of things in the world today, we are very deeply impressed, and oppressed, with the prevailing malady of spiritual blindness. It is the root malady of the time. We should not be far wrong if we said that most, if not all, of the troubles from which the world is suffering, are traceable to that root, namely, blindness. The masses are blind; there is no doubt about that. In a day which is supposed to be a day of unequalled enlightenment, the masses are blind. The leaders are blind, blind leaders of the blind. But in a very large measure, the same is true of the Lord's people. Speaking quite generally, Christians are to-day very blind.

A General Survey of the Ground of Spiritual Blindness

The passages which we have just read cover in a general way a great deal, if not all, of the ground of spiritual blindness. They begin with those who never have seen, those born blind.

Then there are those who have been given vision, but are not seeing very much, nor very clearly - "men as trees walking" - but who come to see yet more perfectly under a further work of grace.

Then there are those who have true and clear sight as far as it goes, but for whom a vast realm of Divine thought and purpose still waits upon a fuller work of the Holy Spirit. *"That He would grant unto you a spirit of wisdom and revelation in the knowledge of Him; having the eyes of your heart enlightened, that ye may know what is the hope of His calling, what the riches of the glory of His inheritance in the saints, and what the exceeding greatness of His power to us-ward who believe."* Those words are addressed to people who have sight, but for whom this great realm of Divine meaning still waits upon their knowing a fuller work of the Holy Spirit in the matter of spiritual sight.

Then, again, there are those who have seen and have followed, but who have lost spiritual sight, of which they were once possessed, and are now blind, but with the most fatal additional factor: they think they see and they are blind to their own blindness. That was the tragedy of Laodicea.

Furthermore, there are those two classes represented by Balaam and Saul of Tarsus, both whom we have quoted. Balaam, blinded by gain, or the prospect of gain. That is, I think, what is meant in the New Testament by following in the way of Balaam; being taken up so much with the question of gain and loss as to be blind to the great thoughts of God and purpose of God, not seeing the Lord Himself in the way, and by his blindness coming very near to being smitten down on the road. The statement is quite definite there - Balaam did not see the Lord until the Lord opened his eyes, then he saw the Lord. "The angel of the Lord", that is the way which it is put. I have not much doubt but that it is the Lord Himself. Then he saw. Later he made that double statement about the matter - "the man whose eye is opened," "falling down and having his eyes open." Such is Balaam, a man blinded by considerations of a personal character, of a personal nature, how things would affect him. That is what it amounts to. And what a blinding thing that is where spiritual matters are concerned. If ever you or I pause on that question, we are in very grave peril. If ever for a moment we allow ourselves to be influenced by such questions as, how will this affect me, what will this cost me, what do I stand to get out of this or to lose by this? That is a moment when darkness may very well take possession of our hearts and we go in the way of Balaam.

Then, on the other hand we have Saul of Tarsus. There is no doubt about his blindness; but his was the blindness of his very religious zeal, his zeal for God, his zeal for tradition, his zeal for historic religion, his zeal for the established and accepted thing in the religious world. It was a blind zeal about which afterward he had to say, *"I verily thought that I ought to do many things contrary to the name of Jesus of Nazareth" (Acts 26:9).* "I thought that I ought." What a tremendous turn around it was when he discovered that the things which he thought, and passionately thought he ought to do in order to please God and to satisfy his own conscience, were utterly and diametrically opposed to God and the way of right and truth. What blindness! Surely he stands as an abiding warning to us all that zeal for anything is not necessarily a proof that the thing is right, and that we are on the right road. Our very zeal as a thing in itself may be a blinding thing, our devotion to tradition may be our blindness. I think eyes have a very large place in Paul's life. When his eyes spiritually were opened, his eyes naturally were blinded, and you can use that as a metaphor. The using of natural eyes religiously may be just the indication of how blind we are, and it may be that, when those natural eyes religiously are blinded, we will see something, and not until they are do we see something. For a lot of people, the thing that is in the way of their real seeing is that they see too much and see in the wrong way. They are seeing with natural senses, natural faculties of reason and intellect and learning, and all that is in the way. Paul stands to tell us that sometimes in order really to see, it is necessary to be blinded. Evidently that left its mark upon him, just as the finger of the Lord left its mark upon Jacob, for the rest of his days. He went into Galatia and later wrote the Letter to the Galatians; and you remember he said, *"I bear you witness, that, if possible, ye would have plucked out your eyes and given them to me"* *(4:15)*; meaning that they noted his affliction, they were aware of that mark which had lasted from the Damascus road, and so felt for him, that if they could have done so, they would have plucked out their very eyes for him. But it is wonderful that the commission which came when he was naturally blinded on the Damascus road was all about eyes. He was blind, and they led him by the hand into Damascus; but the Lord had said in that hour, *"to whom I send thee to open their eyes, that they may turn from darkness to light and from the power of Satan unto God"*.

Well, all these have their own message for us, but they cover the ground fairly generally in relation to spiritual sight. There are, of course, many details, but we will not seek to search those out at the moment; we will get on with this general consideration.

Spiritual Sight, Always a Miracle

When we have covered the whole ground in a general way, we come back to notice one particular and peculiar feature in every case, and that is, that spiritual sight is always a miracle. That fact carries with it the whole significance of the coming into this world of God's Son. The very justification of the coming into this world of the Lord Jesus Christ is found in the Word of God; because it is a settled matter with God Himself that man now is born blind. *"I am come a light into the world"* (John 12:46); *"I am the light of the world"* (John 9:5): and that statement, as you know, was made right there in that section of John's Gospel where the Lord Jesus is dealing with blindness. *"When I am in the world, I am the light of the world", and He illustrates that by dealing with the man born blind.*

Spiritual sight is a miracle from heaven every time, and that means that the one who really sees spiritually has a miracle right at the foundation of his life. His whole spiritual life springs out of a miracle, and it is the miracle of having sight given to eyes which never have seen. That is just where the spiritual life begins, just where the Christian life has its commencement: it is in seeing.

And whoever preaches must have that miracle in his history, and he himself is dependent entirely upon that miracle being repeated in the case of every one who listens to him. That is where he is so helpless and so foolish. Perhaps it is here that, in one sense, we find "the foolishness of preaching". A man may have seen, and may be preaching what he has seen, but no one listening to him has seen or does see: and so he is saying to the blind, See! And they see not. He is dependent entirely upon the Spirit of God coming and, there and then, working a miracle. Unless that miracle is wrought, his preaching is vain, so far as the desired effect is concerned. I do not know what you say when you come into a gathering and bow your head in prayer, but there is a suggestion for you. There may be present that which has come out of a miracle in the one who is giving it forth in preaching or teaching, and you may miss it all. The suggestion is that you ever and always ask the Holy Spirit to work that miracle in you afresh in this hour, that you may see.

But we go further. Every bit of new seeing is a work from heaven. It is not something done fully once for all. It is possible for us to go on seeing and seeing, and yet more fully seeing, but with every fresh fragment of truth, this work, which is not in our power to do, has to be done. Spiritual life is not only a miracle in its inception; it is a continuous miracle in this matter right on to the last. That is what arises from the passages we have read. A man may have had a touch, and, whereas before he was blind and saw nothing, now he sees; but he sees only a little, both in its measure and in its range, and he sees imperfectly. There is a certain amount of distortion about his vision yet. Another touch is required from heaven in order that he may see all things correctly, perfectly. But even then it is not the end, for such as are seeing things correctly, perfectly, within that measure, have yet possibilities from God of seeing such vast ranges. But is it still a spirit of wisdom and revelation which is required to effect it. All the way along it is from heaven. And who would have it otherwise, for is not this the thing which gives to a true spiritual life its real value, that there should forever remain in it the miraculous element?

The Effect of the Loss of Spiritual Sight

Then we come to that final word. To lose spiritual vision is to lose the supernatural feature of the spiritual life, and that produces the Laodicean state. If you seek to get to the heart of this thing, this state of things represented by Laodicea, neither hot nor cold, the state which provokes the Lord to say, "I will spew thee out of My mouth"; if you seek to get to the heart of it and say, Why is this, what is the thing lying behind this? The one thing that explains it is simply this, that it has lost its supernatural feature, it has come down to earth; it is religious, but it has come out of its heavenly place. And then, you see, you get the corresponding rebound to overcomers in Laodicea, "He that overcometh, I will give to him to sit down with Me in My throne". You have gone down a long way to earth, you have lost your heavenly feature, but for overcomers in the midst of such conditions there is still a place above, showing the Lord's thought as over against this condition. To lose spiritual vision is to lose the supernatural feature of the spiritual life. When that has gone out, be as religious as you like, the Lord only has one word to say - Buy eyesalve: that is your need.

The Need of the Hour

That brings us, then, to the need of the hour, the need which, of course, is the need of every hour, of every day, of every age. But we are made more and more aware in our time of this need, and in a sense, we can say there never was a time when there was a greater need for people who could say and can say, I see! That is the need just now. Great and terrible is that need, and not until that need is met will there be any hope. Hope hangs upon this, that there would arise people in this world, this dark world of confusion and chaos and tragedy and contradiction, people who are able to say, I see! If there should arise a man to-day who had position, to exercise influence and be taken account of, and such a man who saw, what new hope would arise with him, what a new prospect! That is the need. Whether that need will be met in a public, national, international way or not, I do not know, but that need must be met in a spiritual way by people on this earth who are in that position, who really can say, I see!

You see, Christianity has so largely become a tradition. The truth has been resolved into truths and put into a Blue-Book, the Blue-Book of Evangelical Doctrine, a set and fenced up thing. These are the evangelical doctrines, they set the bounds of evangelical Christianity in preaching and in teaching. Yes, they are presented in many and various forms. They are served up with interesting and attractive anecdotes and illustrations, and with studied originality and uniqueness, so that the old truths will not be too obvious, but will stand some chance of getting over because of the clothes in which they are dressed up; and a very great deal depends upon the ability and the personality of the preacher or the teacher. People say, I like his style, I like his manner, I like his way of saying things! - and much depends upon that: but when all those trappings have been stripped off, the stories, the anecdotes, the illustrations, and the personality and the ability of the preacher or teacher: when that has all gone, you have simply got again the same old things, and some of us come along and outdo the last man in the way of presenting them in order to gain for them some acceptance, some impression. I do not think that is unkind criticism, for that is what it amounts to; and no one will think that I am asking for a change or dismissal of the old truths.

But what I am trying to get at is this: it is not new truths, it is not the changing of the truth, but it is that there shall be those who, in presenting the truth, can be recognized by those who listen as men who have seen: and that makes all the difference. Not men who have read and studied and prepared, but men who have seen, about whom there is that which we find in this man in John 9 - the element of wonder. "Whether he is a sinner, I know not: one thing I know, that, whereas I was blind, now I see". And you know whether a person has seen or not, you know where it has come from and how it has come: and that is the need: that something, that indefinable something, which works out in wonder, and you have to say, That man has seen something, that woman has seen something! It is that seeing factor which makes all the difference.

Oh yes, it is a far bigger thing than you and I have yet appreciated. Let me tell you forthwith that all hell is banded together against that, and the man who has had his eyes opened is going to meet hell. This man in John 9 was up against it at once. They cast him out, and even his own parents were afraid to take sides with him because of the cost. "He is of age, ask him". Yes, this is our son, but do not press us too much, do not involve us in this thing; go to him, get it cleared up with him, leave us alone! They saw a red light, and so they were seeking to by-pass this issue. It costs to see, and it may cost everything, because of the immense value of seeing to the Lord, and as against Satan, the god of this age, who hath blinded the minds of the unbelieving. It is the undoing of his work. "I send thee to open their eyes, that they may turn from darkness to light and from the power of Satan unto God". Satan is not going to take that, neither at the beginning nor in any measure. It is a tremendous thing, to see.

But oh, what a need to-day for men and women who can stand spiritually in the position in which this man stood and say, I was blind, but now I see, and this one thing I know! It is a great thing to be there. How much I do not know, one thing I do know, I see! Which was not the case before. There is an impact, a registration, with that. Life and light always go together in the Word of God. If a man really sees, there is life, and there is uplift. If he is giving you something secondhand, studied, read, worked up, there is no life in it, other than, perhaps, that temporary and false lift of interest, passing fascination. But there is no real life which makes people live.

So one does not plead for changing the truth or having new truths, but for spiritual sight into the truth. "The Lord hath yet more light and truth to break forth from His Word", which is true. Let me get rid of that thing which has been fastened upon us here if I can. We do not seek for new revelation, and we do not say or suggest or hint that you may have anything extra to the Word of God, but we do claim that there is a vast amount in the Word of God that we have never seen, which we may see. Surely everybody agrees with that: and it is just that - to see, and the more you see, really see, the more overwhelmed you feel about the whole thing, because you know that you have come to the borders of the land of far distances, lying far beyond a short lifetime's power of experience.

Now just to close, let me repeat, that, at every stage from initiation to consummation, spiritual life must have this secret in it, I see! Right at the commencement when we are born again, that should be the spontaneous expression or ejaculation in the life. Our Christian life ought to begin there. But all the way along to the final consummation it must be that, the working out of this miracle, so that you and I are maintained in this atmosphere of wonder, the wonder-factor repeated again and again, so that every fresh occasion is as though we had never yet seen anything at all.

But I may as well say at once that usually a new breaking in of the Spirit in that way follows the eclipse of all that has gone before. It seems that the Lord has to make it necessary, so that we come to the place where we cry out, Unless the Lord shows, unless the Lord reveals, unless the Lord does a new thing, all that ever has been is as nothing, it will not save me now! Thus He leads us into a dark place, a dark time. We feel that what has been has lost the power which it once had to make us buoyant, triumphant. That is the Lord's way of keeping us moving on. If you and I were allowed to be perfectly satisfied with what we have got at any stage, and not to feel the absolute necessity for something we never have had, should we go on? Of course not! To keep us going on, the Lord has to bring about those experiences where it is absolutely necessary for us to see the Lord, and know the Lord in a new way, and it must just be so all the way along to the end. It may be a series of crises of seeing and seeing again, and yet again, as the Lord opens our eyes, and we are able to say, as never before, I see! So it is not our study, our learning, our book knowledge, but it is a spirit of wisdom and revelation in the knowledge of Him, the eyes of our hearts being enlightened, and it is that seeing which brings the note of authority that is so much needed. That is the element, the feature, that is required to-day. It is not just seeing for seeing's sake, but it is to bring in a new note of authority.

Where is the voice of authority today? Where are those who are really speaking with authority? We are languishing terribly in every department of life for the voice of authority. The Church is languishing for want of a voice of spiritual authority, want of that prophetic note - Thus saith the Lord! The world is languishing for want of authority, and that authority is with those who have seen. There is far more authority in the man born blind seeing, in his testimony - One thing I know that, whereas I was blind, now I see - than there is in all Israel, with all Israel's tradition and learning. And may it not be that that was the thing about the Lord Jesus that carried such weight, for "He spoke as One having authority, and not as the Scribes" (Matt. 7:29). The Scribes were the authorities. If anybody wanted an interpretation of the law, they went to the Scribes. If they wanted to know what the authoritative position was, they went to the Scribes. But He spoke as One having authority, and not as the Scribes. Wherein lay that authority? Just that in all things He could say, I know! It is not what I have read, what I have been told, what I have studied, that is with power, but this - I know! I have seen!

The Lord make us all to be of those who have eyes opened.

Chapter 6

The Issue of Spiritual Sight

Reading: Num. 24:3-4; Mark 10:46, 51-52; 8:23-25; John 9:1, 7, 25; Eph. 1:17-19; Rev. 3:17; Acts 26:17-18.

At the outset of our previous meditation we were speaking of the root-malady of our time, which is spiritual blindness. We took those passages which we have read and noted how they, in a very general way, cover the full ground of spiritual blindness and spiritual sight. Then we went on to speak about the common factor in all these cases, which is that spiritual sight is always a miracle. No one has real spiritual sight by nature. It is something which comes out of heaven as a direct act of God, a faculty which is not there naturally, but has to be created. So that the very justification for Christ's coming from heaven into this world is found in this fact, that man is born blind and needed a visitant from heaven to give him sight. Then, finally, to lose spiritual sight is to lose the miraculous element in the Christian life; which was the trouble with Laodicea. We went on to see that the great need of the hour is for those who really can say, I see! Imagine yourself being born blind and living perhaps to maturity without having seen anything or anyone, and suddenly having your eyes opened to see everything and everyone. The sense of wonder would be there; the world would be a wonderful world. I suppose when that man in John 9 went home, he would be constantly saying, It is wonderful to see people, wonderful to see all these things! Wonderful! That would be the word most on his lips.

Yes, but there is a spiritual counterpart, and the great need is of people who have that spiritual wonder in their hearts all the time; that which has broken upon them by revelation of the Holy Spirit and is a constant and ever-growing wonder. It is a new world, a new universe. That is the need of the time - I see!

Well now, the final phase of our afternoon meditation was that which we are going to follow up a little now, that at every stage of the Christian life from initiation to consummation, the secret must just be that - I see: I never saw as I see now! I never saw it like that, I never saw it on this wise; but now I see! It must be like that all the way through, from start to finish, if the life is a true life in the Spirit. So for a little while let us think on one or two phases of the Christian life which must be governed by this great reality of seeing by Divine operation; and you will be recalling a great deal of the Word as I speak, seeing how much there is in the Scriptures about this matter.

Seeing Governs the Beginning of the Christian Life

What is the beginning of the Christian life? It is a seeing. It must be a seeing. The very logic of things demands that it shall be a seeing; for this reason, that the whole of the Christian life is to be a progressive movement along one line, to one end. That line and that end is Christ. That was the issue with the man born blind in John 9. You will remember how, after they cast him out, Jesus found him, and said to him, "Dost thou believe on the Son of God?" and the man answered and said, "And who is He, Lord, that I may believe on Him?" Jesus said unto him, "Thou hast both seen Him and He it is That speaketh with thee." And he said, "Lord, I believe." And he worshipped him. The issue of spiritual sight is the recognition of the Lord Jesus, and it is going to be that all the way through from start to finish.

We may say that our salvation was a matter of seeing ourselves as sinners. But had it been left there it would have been a poor lookout for us.

No, the whole matter is summed up into seeing Jesus, the Christ: and when you really see Christ, what happens? What happened to Saul of Tarsus? Well, a whole lot of things happened, and mighty things which nothing else would have accomplished. You would never have argued Saul of Tarsus into Christianity; you would never have frightened him into Christianity; you would never have either reasoned or emotionalized him into being a Christian. To get that man out of Judaism needed something more than could have been found on this earth. But he saw Jesus of Nazareth, and that did it. He is out, he is an emancipated man, he has seen. Later, when he is right up against the great difficulty of the Judaizes, tracking and following him everywhere to disturb the faith of his converts, to wreck their position in Christ, and they are inclined to fall away, if they have not already done so (I speak of those converts and churches in Galatia), he once again raises the whole question as to what a Christian is, and focuses it upon this very point of what happened on the Damascus road. The Letter to the Galatians really can be summed up in this way: a Christian is not one who does this and that and another thing which is prescribed to be done; a Christian is not one who refrains from doing this and that and another thing because they are forbidden; a Christian is not one at all who is governed by the externalities of a way of life, an order, a legalistic system which says, You must, and You must not: a Christian is comprehended in this saying, "It pleased God to reveal His Son in me:" (Gal. 1:15-16). That is only another way of saying, He opened my eyes to see Jesus, for the two things are the same. The Damascus road is the place. "Who art Thou, Lord?" "I am Jesus of Nazareth." "It pleased God to reveal His Son in me." That is one and the same thing. Seeing in an inward way: that makes a Christian. "God... hath shined in our hearts, to give the light of the knowledge of the glory of God in the face of Jesus Christ" (2 Cor. 4:6). "In our hearts": Christ, so imparted and revealed within, is what makes a Christian, and a Christian will do or not do certain things, not at the dictates of any Christian law, any more than Jewish, but as led by the Spirit inwardly, by Christ in the heart. It is that which makes a Christian, and in that the foundation is laid for all the rest, right on to the consummation, because it is just going to be that growingly. So the foundation must be according to the superstructure; they are all of a piece. It is seeing, and it is seeing Christ.

That is a bold statement upon which a very great deal more might be said. But it is a challenge. We have to ask ourselves now, on what foundation does our Christian life rest? Is it upon something outward; something we have read, something we have been told, something we have been commanded, something we have been frightened into, or emotionalized into; or is it based upon this foundation. "It pleased God to reveal His Son in me"? When I saw Him, I saw what a sinner I am, and I saw too what a Savior He is: but it was seeing Him that did it! I know how elementary that is for a conference of Christians, but it is good sometimes to examine our foundations. We never get away from those foundations. We are not going to grow up and be wonderful folk who have left all that behind. It is all of a piece. I do not mean that we stay at elementary things all our lives, but we take the character of our foundation through to the end. The grace which laid the foundation will bring forth the topstone with shoutings of Grace, Grace! It will all be that; the grace of God in opening our eyes. I will not stay longer with that.

Seeing Governs Spiritual Growth

Let us pass on to growth. Just as the beginning is by seeing, so is growth. Spiritual growth is all a matter of seeing. I want you to think about that. We have to see if we would grow. What is spiritual growth? Well now, answer that carefully, in your heart. I think some people imagine that spiritual growth is getting to know a great deal more truth. No, not necessarily. You may increase in such knowledge as you grow it is true, but it is not just that. What is growth? Well, it is conformity to the image of God's Son. That is the end, and it is toward that that we are progressively and steadily and consistently to move. Full growth, spiritual maturity, will be our having been conformed to the image of God's Son. That is growth. Then if that be so, Paul will say to us, "We all, with unveiled face beholding as in a mirror the glory of the Lord, are transformed into the same image from glory to glory, even as from the Lord the Spirit" (2 Cor. 3:18). Conformity by seeing, growth by seeing.

The Ministry of the Holy Spirit

Now that contains a very precious and deep principle. How can we illustrate? That very passage which we have just cited helps us, I think. The last clause will give us our clue - "as from the Lord the Spirit". I trust I do not use too hackneyed an illustration in trying to help this out when I go back to Eliezer, Abraham's servant, and Isaac and Rebekah, that classic romance of the Old Testament. You remember the day came when Abraham, getting old, called his faithful household steward, Eliezer, and said, 'Put now your hand under my thigh, and swear that you will not take of the women of this country for a bride for my son, but that you will go to my own kith and kin'. And he sware. And then Eliezer set out, as you know, with the camels for the distant Country across the desert, praying as he went that the Lord would prosper him and give him a sign. The sign was given at the well. Rebekah responded to the man, and when, after tarrying a bit and being confronted with the challenge quite definitely, she decided to go with the man, on the way he brought out from his treasures things of his master's house, things of his master's son, and showed them to her, and occupied her all the time with his master's son and the things which indicated what a son he was, and what possessions he had and what she was coming into; and this went on right across the desert until they reached the other side and came into the district of the father's home. Isaac was out in the field meditating: and they lifted up their eyes and saw; and the servant said, "There he is! The one of whom I have been speaking to you all the time, the one whose things I have been showing you: there he is!" And she lighted down from the camel. Do you think she felt strange, as though she had come from a far country? I think the effect of Eliezer's ministry was to make her feel quite at home, to make her feel that she knew the man she was going to marry. She felt no strangeness or distress or foreign element about this thing. They just merged, shall we say? It was the consummation of a process.   "As from the Lord the Spirit." The Lord Jesus said, "When He is come... He shall take of Mine, and show it unto you". "He shall not speak of Himself; but what things soever He shall hear, these shall He speak... He shall take of Mine, and shall show it unto you" (John 16:13-14). The Spirit, the faithful servant of the Father's house, has come right across the wilderness to find the bride for the Son, of His own kith and kin. Yes, there is room for wonder here. "Since the children are sharers in flesh and blood, He also Himself in like manner partook of the same" (Heb. 2:14). "Both He that sanctifieth and they that are sanctified are all of one" (Heb. 2:11). The Spirit has come to secure that bride now, one with Him, His flesh and His bone. But the Spirit desires to be occupying us with the Lord Jesus all the time, showing us His things. To what effect? That we shall not be strangers when we see Him, that we shall not feel that we are of one kind and He another, but that it may just be, 'This is the last step of many which have been leading to this, and every step has been making this oneness more perfect, this harmony more complete'. At the end, without any very great crisis, we just go in. We have been going in all the time, and this is the last step. That is conformity to His image, that is spiritual growth; getting to know the Lord, and to become like Him, getting to be perfectly at home with Him, so that there is no clash, no strangeness, no discord, no distance. Oneness with our Lord Jesus deepening all the time unto the consummation: that is spiritual growth. You see, it is something inward again, and it is but the development of that initiation, that beginning. We have seen and are seeing, and seeing and seeing, and as we see we are changed.

Is that true of everything you think you see? We have to test everything we think we see and know by its effect in our lives. You and I may have an enormous amount of what we think to be spiritual knowledge; we have all the doctrines, all the truths. We can box the compass of evangelical doctrine; and what is the effect? It is not seeing, beloved, in a true spiritual sense, if we are not changed. Yes, seeing is to be changed, and it is not seeing if it does not bring that about. It would be far better for us to be stripped of all that and to be brought right down to the point where we really do see just a little that makes a difference. We must be very honest with God about this. Oh, would we not sooner have just a very little indeed that was a hundred per cent effective, than a whole mountain of knowledge, ninety per cent of which counted for nothing? We must ask the Lord to save us from advancing beyond spiritual life, advancing, I mean, with knowledge, a kind of knowledge, presuming to know. You know what I mean. Real seeing, Paul says, is being changed, and being changed is a matter of seeing as by the Lord the Spirit. So we will pray to see.

Some of us knew our Bible, knew our New Testament, knew Romans, knew Ephesians, thought we saw. We could even lecture on the Bible and these books, and on the truths in them, and did so for years. Then one day we saw; and people saw that we saw, and said, What has happened to the minister? He is not saying anything different from what he has always said, but there is a difference; he has seen something! That is it!

Seeing Governs Ministry

And of course that must lead us to the next thing, though in a very brief word. What is true of the beginning of the Christian life, and what is true of growth, is true in the matter of ministry. Now, do not think I am speaking to any particular class of people called "ministers". Ministry, as we have said here before, is a matter of spiritual helpfulness. Any ministry which is not a matter of spiritual helpfulness is not true ministry, and anybody who is spiritually helpful is a minister of Christ. So we are all in the ministry, in God's plan. Now, since that is so, we are all affected, we are all governed by this same law. To be spiritually helpful is a matter of seeing. You know that 2 Corinthians is the letter in the New Testament which has most to do with ministry. "Seeing we have this ministry" (4:1) - and what is this ministry? Well, "God hath shined into our hearts" (4:6). It is very familiar to us that Paul has at the back of his mind as he writes this part of the letter, Moses, the minister of God. That is the designation by which we know Moses, as the servant of God, and Paul is referring to Moses fulfilling his ministry, his service, reading the law and having to put a veil upon his face because of the glory, the people being unable to look upon him. And that was a glory that was passing. Now, says Paul, in the ministry committed to us God hath shined inside and we have no need of a veil; in Christ the veil is taken away; and what you are to see is Christ in us, and Christ is to be ministered through us as He is seen, as we are the vehicles of bringing Christ into view. That is spiritual helpfulness, that is ministry, namely, bringing Christ into view, and "we have this treasure in vessels of fragile clay, that the exceeding greatness of the power may be of God, and not from ourselves" (4:7). "We are...": and then follows a whole list of things which put us at a discount. But he is saying, in effect, "It is Christ"! If we are put at a discount, if we are persecuted, pursued, cast down, always bearing about in the body the dying of the Lord Jesus, that is only God's way of bringing Christ into view. If we are pursued and persecuted and cast down and the grace of the Lord Jesus is sufficient, and you see the grace of the Lord Jesus being exhibited in that suffering and trial, then you say, that is a wonderful Christ! You see Christ, and by our sufferings Christ is ministered. That is spiritual helpfulness.

Who has helped you most? I know who has helped me most. It has not been anyone in the pulpit. It was one who passed through intense and terrible suffering for many years, and in whom the grace of God was sufficient. I was able to say, "If I go through suffering like that, then mine will be a Christianity worth having, mine will be a Christ worth having." That helped me most, that is what I want to see. Do not preach to me; live, and you help me most. It is an inspiration, surely, or should be to us, to see that it is in our trial and adversity that others may see the Lord and be most helped. How we go through trial is the thing that is going to help someone else better than all that we can say to them. Oh, the Lord cover us as we say a thing like that, for we know our frailty, how we fail Him under trial. But that is what Paul is saying here about ministry. "We have this treasure in vessels of fragile clay... we are persecuted, pursued, cast down, always bearing about in the body the dying of the Lord Jesus." But, with Paul, the end of all such things was, "they glorified God in me" (Gal. 1:24). What do you want more than that? That is ministry. If you and I could say that at any time, well, we should not have lived in vain. We should have been of some help if it could be said, "They glorified God in me."

But it is seeing; we, to be spiritually helpful, have to see, that others may have the ground provided for seeing. I put it that way; because we may see, and we may give out what we see, we may be living epistles, but others may not be seeing. But there is the ground for their seeing, and if they are honest in heart and unprejudiced, really open to the Lord, He will give them to see what it is the Lord has revealed to us and in us, and is seeking to reveal of Himself through us. He must have living epistles, men and women in whom He can be read. That is ministry.

Well, ministry to be given and to be received, is all a matter of this Divine work of grace of opening eyes. I think we can leave it there, and it all constitutes one great appeal to our hearts to seek the Lord to have our eyes opened. It is never too late to get spiritual sight, however blind we may have been, and for however long, if we really mean business with the Lord. But do not forget that this is a matter of being honest with God. The Lord Jesus said a wonderful thing to Nathanael. Nathanael was perilously near that double blindness. At the moment when he allowed himself to give expression to a popular prejudice, he was very near the danger zone. He said, "Can any good thing come out of Nazareth?" That is a popular prejudice. A popular prejudice has robbed many a man and woman of knowing God's fuller thoughts. Prejudices may take many forms. Let us be careful. But Nathanael was saved. The Lord Jesus said, "Hereafter ye shall see the heaven opened, and the angels of God ascending and descending upon the Son of man" (John 1:51). "Hereafter..." - He meant, of course, in the day of the Spirit. "As by the Lord the Spirit", Nathanael would see. Well, he was in danger, but he escaped.

If you are in danger through your prejudice, beware; forsake your prejudice, be open-hearted. Be an Israelite in whom there is no Jacob, no guile, open-hearted to the Lord, and you will see.

Chapter 7

Seeing the Lord and Seeing Ourselves

And all the people of Judah took Uzziah, who was sixteen years old, and made him king in the room of his father Amaziah. He built Eloth, and restored it to Judah, after that the king slept with his father. Sixteen years old was Uzziah when he began to reign; and he reigned fifty and two years in Jerusalem: and his mother's name also was Jechiliah of Jerusalem. And he did that which was right in the eyes of Jehovah, according to all that his father Amaziah had done. And he set himself to seek God in the days of Zechariah, who had understanding in the vision of God: and as long as he sought Jehovah, God made him to prosper (2 Chron. 26:1-5).

But when he was strong, his heart was lifted up, so that he did corruptly, and he trespassed against Jehovah to burn incense upon the altar of incense. And Azariah the priest went in after him, and with him fourscore priests of Jehovah, that were valiant men: and they withstood Uzziah the king, and said unto him, It pertaineth not unto thee, Uzziah, to burn incense unto Jehovah, but to the priests the sons of Aaron, that are consecrated to burn incense: go out of the sanctuary; for thou hast trespassed; neither shall it be for thine honor from Jehovah God. Then Uzziah was wroth; and he had a censer in his hand to burn incense; and while he was wroth with the priests, the leprosy brake forth in his forehead before the priests in the house of Jehovah, beside the altar of incense. And Azariah the chief priest, and all the priests, looked upon him, and, behold, he was leprous in his forehead, and they thrust him out quickly from thence; yea, himself hasted also to go out, because Jehovah had smitten him. And Uzziah the king was a leper unto the day of his death, and dwelt in a separate house, being a leper; for he was cut off from the house of Jehovah: and Jotham his son was over the king's house, judging the people of the land (2 Chron. 26:16-21).

So Uzziah slept with his fathers; and they buried him with his fathers in the field of burial which belonged to the kings; for they said, He is a leper: and Jotham his son reigned in his stead (2 Chron. 26:23).

In the year that king Uzziah died I saw the Lord sitting upon a throne, high and lifted up, and his train filled the temple. Above it stood the seraphim: each one had six wings; with twain he covered his face, and with twain he covered his feet, and with twain he did fly. And one cried unto another, and said, Holy, holy, holy, is Jehovah of hosts: the whole earth is full of His glory. And the foundations of the thresholds shook at the voice of him that cried, and the house was filled with smoke. Then said I, Woe is me! For I am undone; because I am a man of unclean lips, and I dwell in the midst of a people of unclean lips: for mine eyes have seen the King, Jehovah of hosts. Then flew one of the seraphim unto me, having a live coal in his hand, which he had taken with the tongs from off the altar: and he touched my mouth with it, and said, Lo, this hath touched thy lips; and thine iniquity is taken away, and they sin forgiven. And I heard the voice of the Lord, saying, Whom shall I send, and who will go for Us? Then I said, Here am I; send me. And He said, Go, and tell this people, Hear ye indeed, but understand not; and see ye indeed, but perceive not. Make the heart of this people fat, and make their ears heavy, and shut their eyes; lest they see with their eyes, and hear with their ears, and understand with their heart, and turn again, and be healed (Isa. 6:1-10).

This is a very impressive and striking story, and it circles round the matter which has been brought before us at this time, namely, that of spiritual sight. "I saw the Lord"; "mine eyes have seen..."; and everything gathers around that.

What arises from the whole incident is this, that king Uzziah was spiritually and morally a representation of Israel, and of Israel's prophets to a large extent. That is the significance of the double statement by Isaiah the prophet - I am a man of unclean lips, and I am your prophet; and I dwell in the midst of a people of unclean lips. And that, as is very clear, connects with Uzziah; for you know that a leper had to put a cloth upon his upper lip and go about crying, Unclean! The significance of the words: "I am a man of unclean lips, and I dwell in the midst of a people of unclean lips" is just that: we are all lepers. Isaiah is saying, in effect, What was true of Uzziah is true of us all, prophet and people. You do not realize it, and I did not realize it until I saw the Lord. We were all terribly, deeply, impressed with what happened in the case of Uzziah: we have been living in an atmosphere charged with the awfulness of that thing, we have been speaking under our breath about it, saying what a terrible thing it was, what an evil thing Uzziah did, and how awful that our king should turn out to be like that, and have an end like that, what a horrible thing leprosy is; and we have been speaking hard things about Uzziah and thinking many thoughts, how grievous his case was, but I have come to see that we are all in the same case. I, who have been preaching to you (do not forget that five chapters of prophecy have preceded this sixth chapter of Isaiah, this is not the commencement of a preacher's life, but somewhere in his life when he wakes up by a new revelation), I who have been preaching and prophesying, I have come to see that I am no better than Uzziah. You people, going on with your round of religious rites and ceremonies, you attending the temple, you, offering the sacrifices, you, using your lips in worship, you are in the same case as Uzziah: we are all lepers. You may not realize it, but I have come to see. And how have I come to see? I have seen the Lord! "Mine eyes have seen the King, Jehovah of hosts." "I saw the Lord... high and lifted up." I say this is very impressive when you think about it.

Well, what are we going to make of it? Perhaps we would do well just to steal away and be quiet with that a little while, just think it out.

Let us dismiss one thing immediately. It is a popular idea which somehow has sprung up, and by which most of us have been caught, that it was this vision that made Isaiah a prophet or preacher. We have heard that, perhaps we have said that. Oh no! Why, if the Book is inspired and governed by God, should it come long after he had been prophesying so much? Look at those five chapters of prophecies. What tremendous things are in those chapters. No, it was not this that was making him the prophet, the preacher. God was dealing with a man, not a prophet; God was dealing with a people, not with an office. He is getting down to what we are in His own sight. So we cannot just transfer it to a class of people called prophets or preachers, and feel that some of us are not involved because we are not in that class, we are just ordinary simple folk who do not aspire to be prophets and preachers. It is not that. The Lord is getting down to people here and seeking to make clear to them how He views them in themselves, even though they may have been preaching a lot; what they are, after all, in His sight, in themselves. Sooner or later that reality has to break upon us to safeguard everything and to secure His end.

What God is Seeking

What is God after? If you can see, if you can have your eyes opened to see what God is after, then you will understand His method, and why He employs this method. Chapter 5 makes clear what God is after; He is after a people who satisfy His own heart. It is called a remnant. It is called that simply because such a people will be but a remnant. He knows quite well that the whole people will not conform to His thought. He has foreseen that history of His people right up to the days of the coming of His Son, and what this very people will do with His Son. He knows their hearts. That is why He tells Isaiah those terrible things that he is to do: make this people's heart fat, close their ears and their eyes. He knows.

But nevertheless, there will be those who will respond. They will be but a remnant, and that remnant is mentioned specifically at the end of Chapter 6 in these words - *And if there be yet a tenth in it, it also shall in turn be eaten up: as a terebinth, and as an oak, whose stock remaineth, when they are felled; so the holy seed is the stock thereof.*

In the stock that has been felled - and you notice what precedes is the felling of the tree; Israel would be felled by the nations whom God is going to call to cut down Israel, to use as His instruments of judgment, and they would fell this tree of Israel, but the stock will remain - and in the stock, there will be a tenth, there will be a remnant, a holy seed in the stock when the whole tree has been dealt with. God is after a company, even out from the whole general company of His people, who will satisfy His heart, and to secure that remnant. He lays hold of Isaiah and deals with him in this way and gives him this vision. Beloved, in order that God should get His end, we have to be thoroughly disillusioned and have our eyes opened to see very clearly what we are in ourselves in the sight of God. Terrible revelation! Anything which is a suspicion or a suggestion of self-satisfaction, self-complacency, of having attained or being satisfied with our present condition, will disqualify from being in the remnant or in any way instrumental toward God's end, God's purpose.

So, after this man had set out to speak of the wide ranges of the sovereign judgments of God in the first five chapters of Isaiah, suddenly it seems God arrests him. There is a crisis in his own life and in his own ministry. God takes him to the depths of an eye-opening as to what he is, and what the people are, in His sight. He and they who had judged and condemned, and spoken those words with bated breath about the terrible thing that had happened to Uzziah, were shown to be just as bad; there was no difference. In

God's sight, they were all with the cloth upon their upper lips, called upon to cry, "Unclean, unclean"!

The Leprosy of the Self-Life

And what was this leprosy? Oh, we say, of course, sin. Yes, sin; but what is this? Let us have a look at Uzziah and see what leprosy meant, what leprosy represented or betokened in the case of Uzziah. "He did that which was right in the eyes of the Lord, according to all that his father Amaziah had done", and while he walked in the ways of the Lord, the Lord made him to prosper. A man blessed of the Lord, walking in the light of the Lord and knowing the Lord's favor, and, alongside, that deeply rooted thing which is in every man's heart, always ready to rise up and turn the very blessings of God to his own account, to make a name for himself, to get a position for himself, to bring himself aggrandizement and glory and power and influence and satisfaction, to give him a reputation and a position. That is it. What is leprosy? What is this thing which is an abomination to God? It is just that self-life which is in us all, which is ever even coming into the things of God and seeking to make them of personal advantage and account. The Lord blesses, and we become somebody in our own secret hearts because the Lord has blessed. We forget that the very blessings that have come to us have come through grace and the mercy of God, and secretly we begin to think there must be something in us to account for it. It is our ability, our cleverness, something in ourselves. We begin to speak about our blessing, our successes. Oh, it is that thing down there, the leprous germ in us all, the self-life in its manifold ways which produces pride, even spiritual pride, and causes us, like Uzziah, to press in to holy things in self-energy, self-strength, self-assertion, self-sufficiency. Yes, the leprosy is the root of self, selfhood, however it may express itself.

Therein - and it is another branch of things for which we have no time now - therein lies the peril of blessing and prosperity. Oh, how necessary it is for us to be crucified in the midst of our blessings! How necessary it is for God to make safe His blessing of us by continually showing us ourselves, and that it is all of grace, and that if He has given us any kind of blessing, any kind of success, any kind of prosperity at all, it is not because there is something in us in His sight, whatever men may think. Whatever we may be among men, in God's sight we are no better than lepers, and what matters is not how we get on amongst men, but how we get on with God. We might arrive at some very high eminence in this world, but whether we arrive with God or not is the thing that matters.

Now perhaps this goes past most of us, because we are not all too conscious of having been blessed and prospered and having much to boast about. Most of us know the opposite, a good deal of emptying and humiliating. But let us get to the heart of this thing. Even down there in the depths there is a craving in us which is a self-craving, there is a revolt which is the revolt of this self-life. Well, Uzziah is brought to light here in order to show that that is the thing in people and prophet which makes it impossible for God to reach His end; and it has to be dealt with, exposed; it cannot be overlooked; it must be dragged out, and we must see.

The Attainment of God's Object - The Fruit of Seeing the Lord

And so I just come at once and directly to this point, which is that God should get the end upon which His heart is set, a people, though it be but a tenth, a remnant, a people answering to His own heart-desire and satisfying Him in the full purpose of His will. For Him to get that, there must be a seeing, and one thing to be seen, which will do all the rest, is the Lord; and to see the Lord, as this makes so clear, is to see holiness; and when we see holiness we see leprosy where we never suspected it, in ourselves or in others. When we have seen the Lord, we see the true state of things in ourselves and in those around us, even of the Lord's people. To see the Lord is the need, in order that we should be in the way of that end toward which He is pressing.

"I saw the Lord"; "mine eyes have seen". What is the result? Well, it is revealing of ourselves to ourselves, and it is a revealing of the spiritual state around us. When we have seen the Lord, we cry, I am undone! If you look at that word "undone," you will find that it just means this (but this it does mean), I am worthy of death. That is exactly the meaning of the Hebrew word there - worthy of death, I am worthy of death! You and I will see the need for union with Christ in death if our eyes are open to see the Lord; to see that there is nothing else for it, it is the only way.

Now, this is not just language, these are not just words and ideas. What I want us to see is this, for one thing, that the work of the Spirit of God in us, by which our eyes are opened to see the Lord, will result in our feeling that the only thing for us is to die, the best thing for us is to die, to come to an end. Have you got there? Of course, Satan will play on that ground, as indeed he has with many people, trying to drive them to make an end of everything, to work upon something that the Spirit of God is doing and turn it to his own account and create a tragedy. Let us keep in the spiritual realm, and recognize that the Lord will work in us for His own glory and for glorious possibilities, by bringing us to the place where we feel deeply and terribly that the best thing for us is to die. Then He has got us in agreement with His own mind about us. I am undone! - and the Lord might well have said, And so you are: I have known it all the time, I have had difficulty in making you know it; you are undone.

Well, now, when you come to that place, you have come to the place where we can start. While we are there, pressing in all the time, occupying the place like Uzziah, coming into the temple, into the house, into the sanctuary; busy, active; we in ourselves, what we are; while we are filling the temple, the Lord is not able to do anything. He says, Look here, you will have to go out, and you will have to come to the place where you hasten of your own accord to go out because you see you are a leper. That is put in there about Uzziah. "Yea, himself also hasted to go out". At last he realizes that this is no place for him. When the Lord has got us to that place - I am undone, this is no place for me! - then He can start on the positive side, He has the way open. This seeing is a terrible thing, and yet it is a very necessary thing, and in the outcome it is a very glorious thing. The commission came then.

The Reason for the Necessary Experience

I will just add this one thing. Do you see how necessary it was that a thing like that should happen with Isaiah? What was he going to do? Was he going to preach a great revival? Was he going out to tell the people, Everything is all right, the Lord is going to do great things: cheer up, there is a great day just about to dawn? No! God, make this people's heart fat, close their ears, shut their eyes! This is not a very joyful kind of work. What does it amount to? Well you see, the Lord knew the state of the people's hearts. He knows quite well that they do not want to see in reality. In reality they do not want to see. If they wanted to see, oh, they would be taking different attitudes altogether. They would be free of all prejudices, all suspicions, all criticisms; they would be reaching out and inquiring; they would be showing their signs of hunger and longing; they would be investigating, and they would not be readily put off by other peoples' judgments and criticisms. But He knew that in their heart they did not want to see, they really did not want to hear, whatever they might say about it; and this prophet will say later on, "Who hath believed our report?" (Isa. 53:1). The Lord knew, and judgment always comes along the line of a people's heart. If you do not want, you will lose the capacity for wanting. If you do not want to see, you will lose the capacity for seeing. If you do not want to hear, you will lose the capacity for hearing. *Judgment is organic, it is not mechanical.* It comes along the line of our life. You sow a seed of inclination or disinclination and you will reap a harvest of inability, and one effect of a ministry of revelation is to draw out the people's inclination or disinclination unto their own judgment, and you will find that a ministry of revelation and life only makes some people harder. The Lord knows it is there.

Now, to go on with a ministry like that is not a very comfortable thing. You have to be a crucified man to do that, you have to have no personal interest. If you are out for a reputation, for popularity, for success, for a following, then it is best not to go this way, not to see too much, best not to have insight into things; better put blinders on and be an incorrigible optimist. If you are going the way of the Lord's purpose, of a people who really do answer to His thought, it is going to be a way which is cut clean through the mass who will not have it, and who let you know they will not have it, and you go a lonely way. They may think they have a case, but the fact is that they are not hungry and desperate enough even to investigate, to inquire at first hand. They are easily turned aside by the slightest criticism of you, or of your position, of your ministry, and you have to go on with the few, the handful who are going on. It is the price of vision, the price of seeing. Isaiah had to be a crucified man in order to fulfill a ministry like that, and in order for you and me to occupy a position with God, we have to be crucified to that which was in Uzziah, a craving for position. Not satisfied with kingship, he must have priesthood. Nay, more than that, not satisfied with the blessing of God, he must have the very place of God. What a contrast is this! - on the one hand, king Uzziah; on the other, "mine eyes have seen the King."

Can you follow this? It is searching, it is tremendous, but oh, beloved, it is the way of the full desire and thought of the Lord. It is a lonely and costly way, and the effect is really to bring out what God sees in the heart of His people, and in order to do that - which is going to mean that we suffer for our revelation, for our vision, for seeing; we have to pay a great price for it - in order to do that, we have to be well crucified, to come to the place where we say, Well, I am undone, I am deserving of death; there is nothing for it but that I should pass out! The Lord says, That is all right, that is what I want - for you to pass out; I wanted Uzziah to pass out: then I could fill the temple! Uzziah is self, it is man as he is, and God does not co-occupy His house with man, He must fill it.

Chapter 8

The Man who Receives Spiritual Sight

And the angel of the Lord spake unto Philip, saying, "Arise, and go toward the south unto the way that goeth down from Jerusalem unto Gaza, the same is desert." And he arose and went: and, behold, a man of Ethiopia, a eunuch of great authority under Candace, queen of the Ethiopians, who was over her treasure, who had come to Jerusalem to worship; and he was returning and sitting in his chariot, and was reading the Prophet Isaiah. And the Spirit said unto Philip, "Go near, and join thyself to this chariot." And Philip ran to him, and heard him reading Isaiah the prophet, and said, "Understandest thou what thou readest?" And he said, "How can I, except someone guide me?" And he besought Philip to come up and sit with him. Now the passage of the scripture which he read was this, "He was led as a sheep to the slaughter; and as a lamb before his shearer is dumb, so He opened not His mouth: in His humiliation His judgment was taken away: His generation who shall declare? For His life is taken from the earth." And the eunuch answered Philip, and said, "I pray thee, of whom speaketh the prophet this? Of himself, or of some other?" And Philip opened his mouth, and beginning from this scripture, preached unto him Jesus. And as they went on the way, they came unto a certain water; and the eunuch said, "Behold, here is water; what doth hinder me to be baptized?" And he commanded the chariot to stand still: and they both went down into the water, both Philip and the eunuch; and he baptized him. And when they came up out of the water, the Spirit of the Lord caught away Philip; and the eunuch saw him no more, for he went on his way rejoicing. But Philip was found at Azotus: and passing through he preached the gospel to all the cities, till he came to Caesarea (Acts 8:26-40).

In this simple but instructive incident we have three parties. We have the Ethiopian, the Holy Spirit, and the human instrument, Philip. The incident falls into the compass of our present meditation in this Conference concerning spiritual sight.

The Ethiopian

(a) A Confessedly Blind Seeker

When we look at this Ethiopian, we at once see a blind seeker. Though religious, though moving in the circle of long standing and well-established religious tradition, though having been to Jerusalem, to the temple, to the very head-quarters, he is still blind, still a blind seeker. That is quite clear from the questions he put to Philip about the Scriptures of those with whom he was associated, and their prophets. "How can I understand, except someone shall guide me?" "Of whom speaketh the prophet this? Of himself, or of some other?" He is manifestly a man in the dark, a man without spiritual sight, the eyes of his heart have not been enlightened; but the hopeful thing about him is that he is a confessedly blind man.

(b) A Humble Seeker

He was a very important man in this world, a man of considerable responsibility and influence and standing, and because of his position he might well have hedged things a bit. When challenged about his reading, he might have evaded the point or pointedness of the question and have given some kind of evasive non-committal answer. You know how people do who do not like to be thought ignorant, especially if they are people who are regarded as being of some standing, who have a position to keep up. This man, with all that he was amongst men on this earth, was a confessed blind man. Without any hedging or evasion, he answers the question quite directly and honestly and frankly. 'Do I understand what I am reading? Well, how can I except someone teach me?' Then, in his openness, he pressed further for information, for explanation, for enlightenment. "Of whom speaketh the prophet?"

Now, that is very simple, I know, but it is fundamental. It is fundamental to any kind of spiritual understanding, it is basic to all spiritual knowledge, it governs every degree of progress in spiritual things. The humility of this great man is the key to the whole story. He does not seek to give the impression that he knows what he does not know, to lead another to think that he understands when he does not understand; he starts right from the place where he truly and really was. He knew in his own heart that he did not understand and he gave no other impression, but let it be known that was exactly where he was, and that gave a fully opened way to the Lord. May it not be it was this what the Lord had seen long before and upon which He was acting all the time? He knew that He had a perfectly honest and humble man in the dark seeking light, and He could move sovereignly in wonderful ways over considerable distances and take some momentous steps; for these were momentous steps that were taken by the Lord in order to meet that life. You see what such a state of heart makes possible from the Lord's side, how much the Lord is prepared to do when He finds a heart like that. A blind man seeking light, but confessedly blind, and so it is not long before he is an enlightened seeker: for the Lord did not leave such a man in the dark; He gave him the light he was seeking.

And may we not say the Lord gave him a great deal more than he was seeking; for I do not think we should be adding anything to the story if we said that, when he went on his way rejoicing, he felt that he had got a great deal more than he had set out to get. It is always like that. When the Lord does a thing, He does it properly. As Mr. Spurgeon said, "My cup runneth over, and my saucer also! When the Lord does a thing, He does it well". The man went on with a full and overflowing cup, an enlightened seeker. He had come to see what all the religious leaders of his day were not seeking, and were incapable of showing him.

(c) A Seeker Who Meant Business with God

But the enlightenment that came to him brought with it a fresh challenge, as it always does. Every bit of new light coming from the Lord carries with it a fresh challenge, a challenge to some practical obedience. Now I am not going to stay to deal with a most interesting, and I think, a most profitable detail of the whole story, but let us note it. Isaiah 53 brought Christ into view and Philip preached from that scripture Jesus, and the very next thing we strike right up against is, "Here is water; what doth hinder me to be baptized?" Now, you have to do some filling in there, if you are to see how that arises with Isaiah 53. I leave you with that. Do not pass it over: you think about it. All I am going to say is that the revelation which came to the man then, the enlightenment of his eyes, brought with it a challenge to obedience, and this enlightened seeker was not disobedient unto the heavenly vision, but was swift to meet the challenge, quick to run in the way of His command, unhesitant in obedience to the light that had come. So far as the thing itself is concerned, all is very simple; but that is the substance of things. We see a man passing from darkness to light. We see a man passing from a quest to a heart-ravishing knowledge. We see a man fumbling, changed into a man who has a firm grasp, a man whose heart is disappointed changed into one who goes on his way rejoicing. And the two things which from his side make that possible are an utter humility, in that he makes no bones at all about his ignorance and does not feign to know more than he does know, and his swift obedience to light coming to him. You have to say about this man, Here is an honest heart.

And that is how God deals with honest people. They get light and they get joy.

Before we leave him, let us say of him that he is clearly a man who means business. I like this man in his intentness upon knowing and doing. He is right on the mark. All the enervating effect of his Ethiopian climate had not robbed him of spiritual energy. He rose above that, he meant business with God. No element of compromise, excuse, or anything like that at all is found in him. He was simply set upon knowing, if it could be known, and doing whatever there was to be done when enlightened.

Well, to the man who is bent on thus knowing and coming into things, God is going to show Himself of the same kind. God is to us what we are to Him. God will be debtor to no man, and if you and I really mean business with God and are going right out for all that God has for us, all that God wants us to have and to know, and are not going to take on any airs but get right down to the level where we really and genuinely are, in all humility, and we mean that whatever the Lord shows us we are going to do it by His grace without any hesitation, we shall find that, in the long run, God is not going to be our debtor, but He will meet us to the full. This man's story is given an immortal record. It comes in the Acts of the Holy Spirit, and when you come to ask the question, Why is this man included in the record and his story handed down from age to age to last as long as time? The answer is just what we have said: he was a man who meant business with God, was open to the Lord, honest in heart, humble in spirit, and obedient to the light that he had.

The Holy Spirit

(a) The Ground He Requires

Well, then, the second party in the story is the Holy Spirit, and a brief word only needs to be said. Of course, in reality He was the first party in the whole business, but I mention Him second here because it is perhaps more helpful to examine the incident in this order. The Holy Spirit was aware of such a man, and the Holy Spirit is always aware of such a man. There is a sense in which an

Ethiopian must go before the Holy Spirit. You understand what I mean by that. Before the Holy Spirit can really do His work, He must have something upon which to do it that meets His requirements, and the Holy Spirit was cognizant of this man, of his quest and of his heart, and the Holy Spirit is always aware of such people as to where they are.

(b) How He Is Hindered

I think there is a very big story hanging upon a statement like that. If we did but know it, a lot of our problems are solved by understanding that. There is the big question which is always confronting us as to why is it that some leap into the light and go on, and others do not, but always lag behind, and never seem to see any more? Is it that there is a selectiveness on the part of God, a kind of elect of the elect that He has, is it that He has favorites? I do not think so. I think a great part of the answer lies here, namely, in what God finds He has to deal with, whether people mean business with Him or not, whether He has a clear way or not, whether the ground is occupied or not already by that which is an obstruction to Him. I do not think anybody will fail to get all the light the Lord wants them to have if they really do mean business with God. The Holy Spirit knows us. He looks right deep down into our hearts and knows whether we mean business. He sees exactly what there is to hinder Him and how far He can go; for the Lord is not going to coerce anyone. If we are taken up with ourselves, occupied with ourselves, circling round ourselves, centering in ourselves, then the Holy Spirit has not a chance. We have to come to an end of ourselves. That is the trouble with so many. They have got a self-complex set up, and all the time it is a continuous going round in a circle and coming back to the same point at which they started, and it is all round themselves, and they are wearing themselves out. Before long they are going to have an awful crash that involves all that for which they are supposed to stand and represent for the Lord, and it will come down with them. The Holy Spirit has not a clear way. We have to get out of the way, so far as this self-occupation is concerned, if we are going to move straight on, and to go on. He knows exactly where we are, whether we are tied up in them that we are not open to the Lord to consider any further light at all. We have got it all, or our people with whom we are associated have got it all, and we are a part of that! You know what I mean. The Holy Spirit cannot do much with folk who are in a position like that; and He knows. His attitude is, It is no use, I cannot do much there, they are too tied up. But, if we are prepared to put everything into the water, then the Lord can go on and get a clear way.

The Holy Spirit knows. He knows you and He knows me. He knows us a great deal better than we know ourselves. We may have thought that we meant business and have been praying very much a long time and crying to the Lord to do something, while the Holy Spirit knows quite well that we are not at an end of ourselves and our own interests yet. Something more has to be done to bring us to despair before He can do what He wants. But He knows: that is the point. He knew this man. He knew that He had not a great deal to do to make a start with every prospect of a clear way, and He took the opportunity presented, and He was able to act sovereignly. He did that in order to meet this need.

The Human Instrument

Now I do not want to take very much time, so I pass to the third of the three, the human instrument: Philip, the means by which, on the one hand, the blind seeker would have his eyes opened, and by which, on the other hand, the Holy Spirit will be able to accomplish His work. We all want to be in that position where really honest, genuine, business-meaning men and women can find what they are after through our instrumentality if God so will, and, on the other hand, where the Holy Spirit can find in us a vessel to hand where He sees such a need. Surely there is nothing we would desire more than that, just to be as Philip was.

But even in Philip's case, it was not that he was an automatic bit of machinery, something taken up willy-nilly. There were things about Philip which constituted the ground for the Lord; very, very simple matters, and yet not such as are so easy in practical life and outworking.

Philip was at the disposal of the Holy Spirit, and that without any question, and when you look, you see that that meant something in his case. Philip was down there in Samaria. Many were turning to the Lord, a great work of grace was going on, so great a work that they had to send down apostles from Jerusalem to deal with the situation; and Philip was the chief instrument in that work in the first place. Now when you are right in the thing like that, and the Lord suddenly says, "Now, Philip, I want you to leave all this and go down by the way that is desert; I will not tell you why, I will not tell you what I am going to do, I simply say, go to the desert", a man might have big questions. He might have said, But Lord, what about this? But, Lord, look at this big door of opportunity, look what I am doing, what I am in! What will happen here if I leave it? Many questions like that might have arisen. He could have had serious reservations and put them in the way of the Lord. But we do not read of anything like that. The Lord simply said it, and Philip was so much at the disposal of the Lord that, without any questions, he moved. What a tremendous thing it is to be free for the Lord, free to the Lord, to be so much at the Lord's disposal that it is not difficult at all to leave anything, to adjust ourselves to an altogether new situation, if the Lord says it. It is a great thing. So Philip was at the Lord's disposal, and that is a big factor in a work like this of bringing sight to blind seekers, and being, not only the answer to man's need, but the answer to the need of the Holy Spirit; at the Lord's disposal and unhesitating in response to the Lord's suggestion; no delay, but a swift answer. "The Lord has said it, let us get on with it and leave the responsibility with Him."

It turned out all right, it was quite a safe thing to do. Now, the Lord never does explain Himself in advance. The Lord never does tell us ahead how it is going to work out and what He is going to do. He always presents us with a challenge to faith in Him. All His requirements carry with them plenty of opportunities for arguing if you are so disposed; plenty of occasions, humanly speaking, of questions. The one who knows the Spirit knows well that the vindication will come along the line of swift obedience.

Well now, that is the story; simple, beautiful, but containing vital principles of enlightenment. If you want to see people go on, these are the things which the Lord requires. If you want to go on, these are the things which lie behind all real going on, all leaping into light, into knowledge, in the greater fullness of the Lord.

Well, look again at this man. It is a great story. You know that the Bible holds up Ethiopia as a type of darkness: but here is the darkness changed to the light, the full blaze of the noonday; for Christ is that: and that is the basis on which it is done, namely, a heart that is frank, humble, purposeful, and honest in its search.

I do not know what the Lord may be saying to you, but for us all the pivot of the whole matter is, Here is water! I am not saying that baptism is the pivot, but I am saying that it is represented by baptism. Are we ready for everything to go into the grave? Have we something we are holding on to; our position, our reputation, our status and all that, or is it all going into the grave? The Lord here has a man who does not say, "Is it necessary for me to be baptized; must I? Of course, if the Lord requires it, I will seek grace;" but a man who says, "Here it is, what doth hinder?" That is another angle altogether. Tell me anything that hinders and I will deal with it! Get that kind of spirit. 'If you can show me anything that hinders my going on in the way that the Lord indicates, then I will deal with it. What does He want, Philip? Can you tell me of any hindrance?' Philip found no hindrance, but everything to help. Both went down together and Philip baptized him. The Lord just put into our hearts the meaning of that and give us to be good Ethiopians in this spiritual sense.

Chapter 9

The Cause and Ground of Blindness

But if the ministration of death, written, and engraven on stones, came with glory, so that the children of Israel could not look stedfastly upon the face of Moses for the glory of his face; which glory was passing away: how shall not rather the ministration of the spirit be with glory? For if the ministration of condemnation hath glory, much rather doth the ministration of righteousness exceed in glory. For verily that which hath been made glorious hath not been made glorious in this respect, by reason of the glory that surpasseth. For if that which passeth away was glorious, much more that which remaineth is in glory. Having therefore such a hope, we use great boldness of speech, and are not as Moses, who put a veil upon his face, that the children of Israel should not look stedfastly on the end of that which was passing away: but their minds were hardened: for until this very day at the reading of the old covenant the same veil remaineth, it not being revealed to them that it is done away in Christ. But unto this day, whensoever it shall turn to the Lord, the veil is taken away. Now the Lord is the Spirit: and where the Spirit of the Lord is, there is liberty. But we all, with unveiled face beholding as in a mirror the glory of the Lord, are transformed into the same image from glory to glory, even as from the Lord the Spirit. (2 Cor. 3:7-18; A.R.V.).

Therefore, seeing we have this ministry, even as we obtained mercy, we faint not: but have renounced the hidden things of shame, not walking in craftiness, nor handling the word of God deceitfully;

but by manifestation of the truth commending ourselves to every man's conscience in the sight of God. And even if our gospel is veiled, it is veiled in them that perish: in whom the god of this world hath blinded the minds of the unbelieving, that the light of the gospel of the glory of Christ, Who is the image of God, should not dawn upon them. For we preach not ourselves, but Christ Jesus as Lord, and ourselves as your servants for Jesus' sake. Seeing it is God, that said, Light shall shine out of darkness, who shined in our hearts, to give the light of the knowledge of the glory of God in the face of Jesus Christ" (2 Cor. 4:1-6).

We have been led to be concerned with the matter of spiritual sight. Here in the scripture which we have read we have another portion touching upon this very matter of blindness and seeing.

First, there is the fact of the blindness - "the god of this age hath blinded": then there is the cause - "the god of this age"; and then there is the reason or object, namely; "that the light of the gospel of the glory of Christ, Who is the image of God, should not dawn upon them." We will look at it, then, in that order.

The Fact of Blindness

You will notice that a parallel is drawn between Israel in the days of Moses and the unbelieving in the days of Paul. In both cases it is said that there is a veil over their hearts, over their minds, a veil which shuts out, which excludes, and which is in the nature of darkening blindness. Moreover there is an element of judgment and condemnation in the way in which the apostle speaks of it. Even with regard to Israel gathered to the door of the tent of meeting, when Moses read the law, he says, in effect, that while Moses had to put a veil over his face because they could not bear to look upon the glory of his face, that was not really because the glory could not be beheld, but because of the state of their mind, of their heart, because of an inward condition in themselves. Had there been another inward state, the veil would have been unnecessary; they could have beheld the glory and dwelt in the light. But the veil was an outward representation of an inward condition, hiding the glory of God. It was never the Lord's desire to hide His glory, but rather to manifest it, and that man should dwell in it, should enjoy it, that there should be no veil between God and man at all. Veils have always been as something between God and man because of a condition which God would rather not have.

The Blinding Power of Unbelief

Thus it must stand as a thing under condemnation and judgment, this darkness, this blindness, this hiding, this shutting out of the glory of God, and that inward condition in the case of Israel in the time of Moses, and of those in like condition in the days of Paul, and in the case of all in such a position, that inward condition which acts like a veil is, as we know so well from all that is said about Israel, incorrigible unbelief. It was Israel's incorrigible unbelief which blinded them. But to say that is not to be altogether helpful. It is a statement of a fact, a very oppressive fact. We know our own hearts sufficiently well to know that there is an incorrigible unbelief in us all, and we want to understand why that unbelief is there, and what the nature of it is, so as to discover how the veil can be removed; that is, how the unbelief can be dealt with so that we behold the glory of the Lord and dwell in the eternal light.

Light on Resurrection Ground

Well then, let us look again to see what the Lord was ever and always seeking to do in the case of Israel. We can put it this way: He was always trying to get them in heart, in spirit, in life, to occupy resurrection ground. That is first made evident in the Passover in Egypt, when the firstborn in every home in Egypt was slain on that terrible night when death was everywhere. But Israel was not, as is too superficially supposed, exempt. The casual, superficial idea is that the firstborn in Israel were not slain, only the firstborn in Egypt.

But the firstborn in all Israel were slain. The difference was that the firstborn in Egypt were slain actually, and the firstborn in Israel substitutionary. When that lamb was slain in every Israelitish home, for every household, that lamb representatively passed under the same judgment as the firstborn in all Egypt, and in that lamb Israel passed representatively from death into life. In that lamb Israel was virtually brought through death on to resurrection ground. For Egypt there was no resurrection ground; for Israel there was. That is the difference. But all died, the one actually, the other representatively. Thus God, right at the very foundation of Israel's national life, sought to get them established upon the ground of resurrection, which means that a death has taken place, an end has been brought about. One whole order of things has been wound up and another entirely different order of things has been brought in, and to get them to take their position upon that new ground, in that new order, was God's great effort and meaning in the Passover. The keeping of the Passover year by year as an established ordinance throughout all their generations and their history was God's way of showing that they belonged to another order, the order of the resurrection. While darkness was in every house of the Egyptians and over all the land of Egypt, the children of Israel had light in their dwellings; for light is always on resurrection ground, but only on resurrection ground.

Then at the Red Sea the same great principle was repeated, passing through and out on to resurrection ground; Egypt again swallowed up, but Israel saved. They all went into the same sea, but for Israel on the other side there is a pillar of fire to be their light on resurrection ground - the Spirit of light and of life. They kept the Passover as they went on year by year under God's order, in order to preserve the testimony as to the ground upon which they stood nationally.

Then came the Jordan; and it is but a reiteration in the principle of the same thing, now made necessary, not by their naked condition, but by their recognition of it. It is doubtful whether in

Egypt and at the Red Sea Israel had the subjective understanding of the meaning of what God was doing in the Passover and in the Red Sea, but now they have the subjective consciousness of its being a necessity. They have been discovering things for forty years and they agree at last; they agree with God that another ground altogether is necessary if they are to abide in the light. You see, God was persistently by every means seeking to get Israel to occupy and remain upon resurrection ground, from which there had been cut off entirely all the ground of nature. Their incorrigible unbelief had as its main constituent the clinging to unresurrection ground or ground of nature.

The Consequence of Living on the Ground of Nature

What is the ground of nature? Well, look at Israel and you can see quite clearly what the ground of nature is. The ground of nature is always a drawing of things toward oneself and a viewing of everything in the light of oneself, just how it affects self. You see right at the beginning it was that. Yes, of course, the deliverance at the beginning affected us rather well, and so we were very happy. The mighty deliverance at the Red Sea is a good thing for us, so we are full of joy today. It will always be like that while things are good for us. But let us find that we are being tested at all, bring us tomorrow to this place and that, where it is not so obvious that it is all to our profit, and the song ceases, joy goes out, and murmuring comes in "They murmured." Oh how often it is said that they murmured! Why? Because they occupied carnal ground, natural ground, which in a word, means "how it affects me"! That is natural ground, and on that ground there will always be the uprising of unbelief.

The strength of unbelief is just that very thing, personal natural interests and considerations, looking at things in the light of our own advantage or disadvantage. Allow that kind of thing to come in for a moment, and it will not be long before you are questioning and doubting, and found in unbelief; for the essence of faith is the very opposite of that. When things are going against you and your interests, and you are losing your life and all that you have, and you believe God, you trust God, that is faith indeed, that is the essence of faith. But faith is not real faith when we believe God merely while the sun shines and all goes well. Israel occupied natural ground so persistently that they were found more in unbelief than in faith. It was that which blinded them. So that blind unbelief, when we come to analyze it, is simply occupying ground that is other than resurrection ground; that is, we are occupying ground which God has put under the curse, which God has forbidden, upon which God has inscribed the warning to believers, Keep off! If only we could see in our hearts those warning notices of God strewn over the whole territory of self-interest, worldly considerations, and so on, we should be saved from very much of the misery which comes into our lives.

Well, you see, the whole life of nature is a blind thing, and the measure in which we are ruled by nature is the measure of our blindness. "The natural man", says the Spirit of God, "receiveth not the things of the Spirit of God... he cannot know them, because they are spiritually discerned" or "discerned by the spiritual" (1 Cor. 2:14). The whole life of nature is a blind thing. The measure in which we occupy that ground is the measure of our blindness. God was seeking to get Israel off that ground on to resurrection ground, to be governed, not by nature, but by the Spirit: and being governed by the Spirit means to walk in the light, means to have light, means to see.

A Life in the Spirit

"Now the Lord is the Spirit: and where the Spirit of the Lord is, there is liberty" (2 Cor. 3:17). Liberty from what? Why, liberty from the veil. "When it shall turn to the Lord, the veil is taken away"; bondage, limitation, is taken away. And "the Lord is the Spirit". To be on the ground of the Spirit, which is resurrection ground, with the life of nature set aside, is to be delivered from blindness and to be in the light. A life in the Spirit! Israel forever stands to declare with no uncertain note that religion is not necessarily enlightenment, and that even to have the Scriptures is not necessarily enlightenment. "When Moses is read, a veil lieth upon their heart". "When Moses is read..." Paul said a very strong thing about the Scriptures and the prophets which they read every day; that they know not what they mean, perceive not what they signify, but are still in blindness, in darkness. No, even to have the Scriptures does not necessarily imply enlightenment.

The message of 2 Corinthians is as much to Christians as it is to unbelievers, if it is not more so, this message about the veil, about blindness, about seeing; for where is the Christian who is fully and finally delivered from the life of nature? Enlightenment, after all, is only a comparative thing, that is, it is a "more or less" matter. Hence all those strong urges and exhortations to believers to walk in the light, to live in the Spirit, for only so can this matter of spiritual seeing and understanding develop and make progress. A life in the Spirit - that is only another way of saying, a life on resurrection ground.

What we have said thus far is that the blindness which is spread over the whole of the life of nature operates and has its strength in the choice and acceptance of that life of nature on the part of those concerned. It is not necessary; it is not God's will. God's desire is that we should dwell in the light, that we should see His glory, that there should be no veil at all. That is His desire, that the veil should be taken away. But one great thing is necessary, namely, that we should come to that Passover, to that death which is the death to the life of nature and which brings in a new life altogether, a life of the Spirit, in which a new faculty, a new power, a new capacity for seeing is created. That is a very important thing. I could well spend much time on that, it is so important to us as the Lord's people.

When will the Lord's people who have the Scriptures, and who know the Scriptures so well in the letter, when will they come to realize and to recognize that, if truly they have been crucified with Christ, if they have died in His death and have been raised together with Him, and have received the Spirit, they have light in their dwelling? "The anointing which ye received of Him abideth in you, and ye need not that anyone teaches you, but... His anointing teacheth you concerning all things" (1 John 2:27). When will believers, when will Christians, come to realize that? Why must Christians who have the knowledge of the Scriptures in the letter run about here and there to seek advice from others on matters which vitally affect their own spiritual knowledge? I do not mean that it is wrong to get counsel, wrong to know what other children of God of experience think or feel about matters. But if we are going to build our position upon their conclusions, we are in great danger. The final authority and arbiter in all matters is the Spirit of God, the Spirit of the anointing. We may get help from one another, but I do hope that you are not going to build your position upon what I say now because I say it. Do not do that. I do not want you to do it, I do not ask you to do it. What I say is, listen, take note, and then go to your final authority Who is in you, if you are a child of God, and ask Him to corroborate the truth or to show otherwise. That is your right, your birthright, the birthright of every child of God, to be in the light of the indwelling Spirit of light, the Spirit of God.

I wonder where Paul would have been had he taken the opposite course to that which he did take? "When it pleased God, Who separated me from my birth... to reveal His Son in me... straightway I conferred not with flesh and blood: neither went I up to Jerusalem to them that were apostles before me: but I went away into Arabia" (Gal. 1:15-17). I wonder what would have happened had he gone up to Jerusalem and laid every matter before those who were apostles before him? We know from subsequent events that one thing they would have said to him would have been, Look here, be careful, Paul! You tell us that on the Damascus road Jesus is supposed to have said something to you about going to the Gentiles; be careful! They would have put him back about this Gentile business. You know what happened afterward. You know how on that point even Peter was caught in dissimulation years after. You know how those apostles which were before him at Jerusalem were all the time very chary (cautious) about this matter of the Gentiles, and had Paul capitulated to them, we should never have had the great apostle to the Gentiles, the great apostle of the Body of Christ, with his revelation of the mystery, of the oneness of all in Christ, Jew and Greek. He did not submit that thing even to those who were apostles before him to ask them whether he was right or not, whether this was sound or not. Oh no! He had the anointing in Damascus; Ananias laid his hands upon him and he received the Spirit, and from that day, although Paul was quite ready and happy to have fellowship with his brethren, though he never took a superior or independent position, though he was always open to conference, nevertheless he was a man governed by the Spirit.

I know you have to be careful how you take what I am saying. It will only be safe for you as you are one who does not set yourself up as some independent party with the Holy Spirit, but who keeps perfect fellowship, humility, submissiveness, openness of heart, with readiness to listen to and obey what may come through others, as the Spirit bears witness to the truth. But all that depends upon your inward condition, whether you are on natural ground or on spiritual ground, on old creation ground or on resurrection ground. But being on resurrection ground, where it is not the life of nature but the Spirit that governs, beloved, you have the right and the privilege and the blessing of knowing the Spirit bearing witness in your heart and the anointing teaching you all things, with regard to whether any given matter is right or wrong. When will the Lord's people know that, recognize that?

You see, it is this other thing all the time that is robbing so many of the light that the Lord would give them. The Lord would lead them into the greater fullness of the knowledge of His Son, of the enlargement of their spiritual understanding, but they are neglecting the gift that is in them. They are neglecting the Holy Spirit as their illuminator and teacher and instructor and guide and arbiter, and they are going to this one and that one, to this authority and that, and saying, What do you think about it? If you think it is wrong, then I will not touch it! It is fatal to spiritual knowledge to do that. That is going on to natural ground.

Now the Lord wants us off of that ground. This matter of occupying resurrection ground, of living a life in the Spirit, is all-important in coming to the full knowledge of God's Son. How much more we could say about that! Let us be careful as to who our authorities are. So many dear children of God, individually and collectively, have come into dire and grievous bondage, limitation and confusion, by all the time going back to human authorities, to this great leader and that, to this man who was greatly used of God, this man who had a great deal of spiritual light. "The Lord has yet more light and truth to break forth from His Word" than even this or that servant of His possessed. Do you see what I mean? We get all the benefit of the light given to godly people and seek to profit by true light, but we will never come into bondage and say, That is the end of that matter! That must never be. We must maintain our resurrection ground. And who can exhaust that? In other words, who can exhaust the meaning of Christ risen? He is a boundless store, the land of far distances. No man yet has ever done more than begun to know the meaning of Christ risen. If there has been one man who has that meaning more than another, I suppose it was Paul. But to the last from his prison he still cries, "That I may know Him!": "I count all things to be loss for the excellency of the knowledge of Christ Jesus my Lord: for Whom I suffered the loss of all things, and do count them but refuse" (Phil. 3:8). Right at the end of a life like his, the life of a man who could say, Fourteen years ago I knew a man in Christ, caught up to the third heaven and shown unspeakable thing, which, it is not lawful for a man to utter (2 Cor. 12:2-3), he is still saying, That I may know Him! I say no man, not even Paul, has ever done more than begin to know Christ risen. "Eye hath not seen, nor ear heard, neither have entered into the heart of man, the things which God hath prepared for them that love Him. But God hath revealed them unto us by His Spirit" (1 Cor. 2:9-10). You see, the Spirit has the unsearchable riches to reveal to us. So much, then, for the blindness which comes by occupying natural ground in whatever form that may take.

The Cause of Blindness

A word or two about the cause. "The god of this age hath blinded." There are two things in that phrase. Firstly, this blindness is not, after all, only natural, it is supernatural. It is not to say everything to say that nature is a blind realm. No, there is something very much more sinister than that about this blindness. It is supernatural blindness, but it is evil supernatural blindness. It is the work of the Devil. That is why, on the one hand, spiritual sight-giving is always fraught with such terrible conflict. No one ever really does come to see by the Spirit and understand without a fight, without a price having to be paid, without a terrible amount of suffering. Every bit of real spiritual illumination and enlightenment is a costly thing. For it Paul had to be much on his knees where the saints were concerned. "I bow my knees"; I pray "that the God of our Lord Jesus Christ, the Father of glory, may give unto you a spirit of wisdom and revelation in the knowledge of Him" (Eph. 1:17). It is something which has to be prayed through, and it is not without significance that prayer in the Letter to the Ephesians comes so much in association with what is revealed in chapter 6: "our wrestling... is against the principalities, against the powers, against the world-rulers of this darkness, against the spiritual hosts of wickedness in the heavenlies. Wherefore take up the whole armor of God" - this and that and that - "...with all prayer and supplication praying at all seasons in the Spirit" (Eph. 6:12-18). "This darkness" - "praying always": "I pray that He... may give unto you a spirit of wisdom and revelation in the knowledge of Him". You see, it is all of a piece. The explanation lies here, in "the god of this age". We are up against something supernatural in this spiritual blindness. We are right up against the whole cosmic forces of evil, all those intelligences operating to keep people in blindness.

It is no small thing to have true spiritual sight. It represents a mighty victory. It is not going to come to you by just sitting passively and opening your mouths for it to arrive. There has to be exercise about this matter. You are right up against the full force of the god of this age when you are really out for spiritual understanding. It is a supernatural battle. So every bit of ministry that is going to be a ministry of true revelation will be surrounded by conflict. Conflict will go before, conflict will go on at the time, and conflict may follow after. It is like that.

Herein, then, is the need for you to be exercised about light, that, while you hear the thing, you shall not take it for granted that, having heard it, you have got it; that you should afterward have very definite dealings with the Lord, that what He is seeking to break through to you shall indeed be entered into, and that you are not going to delude yourself by assuming that you know now merely because you have heard it in its terms. You may not know it. It may not yet be delivering light; there may be a battle necessary in this matter.

If we did but know it, a very great deal of the conflict which arises in our lives is because God is seeking to bring us further on the road, to open our eyes to Himself, to bring us into the light of His Son. God is seeking to broaden our spiritual horizon, and the enemy is out against that, and he is not going to have it if he can help it. Conflict arises. We may not understand it, but very, very often, more often than not, it is just that, namely, that the Lord is after something, and Satan says, They shall not see that if I can help it! So there arises a mighty warfare. This blindness is supernatural, just as enlightenment is supernatural.

"The god of this age"! That designation may mean more than just a period in time. It may mean all of time, because Satan gained kingship over man right at the beginning. That is what he was after, to take the place of God and to get the worth-ship of man's life; to be god, to be worshipped; which simply means to take what man has of worth to himself. God made man with a view to his being a vehicle of bringing something to God for God's pleasure and glory, something worthy of God, that God should have a worth-ship out of man, and Satan said: I am going to have that worth-ship; God has something vested in that creation, something He is going to get for Himself; I am going to have it! So the whole of what took place in the Garden was Satan's way of supplanting God in man's heart, in man's mind, and getting from man that which was God's right - the worship. Thus, by man's consent and fall, Satan gained godship in this world, and has held it ever since. "This age" just means the course of this world. "The god of this age"!

Now, the greatest peril to Satan's godship is spiritual illumination. He will not hold that ground long once your eyes are opened. Oh, once a heart is enlightened, Satan's power is at once broken. So the Lord, consistently with that fact, said to Paul on the Damascus road - "...unto whom I send thee, to open their eyes, that they may turn from darkness to light and from the power of Satan unto God" (Acts 26:17-18). The two things go together: From darkness to light; from the power of Satan unto God. I repeat that the greatest menace and peril to Satan and his position is spiritual illumination. Hence he must find ground on which to perpetuate and maintain his position, his godship, in this age. And what ground will satisfy him in that matter? The answer is, the ground of nature. You get on to the ground of nature and you have given Satan right of possession. Every time we do that, Satan's hold is strengthened.

The Object of the Blinding Work of Satan

Now just to mention and hint at the third thing. What is the reason or object of this blinding work of Satan? It is that "the light of the gospel of the glory of Christ, Who is the image of God, should not dawn upon them" (2 Cor. 4:4). The glory of Christ; the gospel of the glory of Christ; the light of the gospel of the glory of Christ; Who is the image of God; lest that should dawn upon them, and that it should not dawn upon them, the god of this age hath blinded them.

Then what is the object? We are taken back to some dateless time when in the counsels of the Godhead the Son was appointed heir of all things. He Who was co-equal with God was put in the way of inheriting all things. When that was known in heaven, there was one in the angelic hosts in whose heart iniquity was found. That iniquity was the pride of desiring that equality and aspiring to that inheritance. His heart was lifted up, and he said, "I will exalt my throne above the stars of God... I will be like the Most High" (Isa. 14:12-14; Eze. 28:11-19), in the saying of which he uncovered his jealousy of God's Son; and out from that iniquity of his heart, that pride, that jealousy of his heart, he lost his place there, and he has come down and pursued his course of animosity all through the ages, that men shall never see the Son if he can help it. That the light of the glory of Christ should not dawn upon them, he has darkened and blinded them. It is to exclude the Son.

That surely signifies something immense where Christ is concerned, if Satan, with all his great intelligence and understanding, recognizes that, if men see that Son, it is the greatest thing that ever could happen. Everything of God's intention is bound up with that. All God's great purpose in the creation of this world, and this universe, hangs upon that. It is all vested in the Son, and if men see the Son, then God reaches His end and realizes His purpose. Satan says, That must not be, they must not see the Son! The god of this age hath blinded their minds, lest the light of the glory of Christ, Who is the image of God, should dawn upon them.

What a thing it is to see the Son then! I cannot stay now with that immense matter. But let us finish on this note: What a tremendous shout will go up throughout the universe when at last we see Him face to face, when there is no more darkening veil at all in any degree. God has His end then; the Son appears, the Son is seen. When we see Him, "we shall be like Him; for we shall see Him even as He is" (1 John 3:2). That is what God made us for: "fore-ordained to be conformed to the image of His Son" (Rom. 8:29). But oh, seeing now and seeing evermore unto the perfect day is necessary, for it is as we behold that we are changed into that image.

What is the prayer upon our lips and in our hearts as we go away? Let it not be mere sentiment, let it be a persistent cry and a persistent quest - We would see Jesus! In the seeing of Him all the purpose of God in this universe is bound up.

Chapter 10

Seeking the Glory of Christ as Son of God

God... hath at the end of these days spoken unto us in His son, Whom He appointed Heir of all things (Heb. 1:1-2; A.R.V.).

... the kingdom of His Son... Who is the image of the invisible God, the Firstborn of all creation; for in Him were all things created, in the heavens and upon the earth, things visible and things invisible, whether thrones or dominions or principalities or powers; all things have been created through Him, and unto Him; and He is before all things, and in Him all things consist (Col. 1:13-17).

...the glory of Christ... we preach... Christ Jesus as Lord (2 Cor. 4:4-5).

In the beginning was the Word, and the Word was with God, and the Word was God... All things were made through Him; and without Him was not anything made that hath been made. In Him was life; and the life was the light of men (John 1:1, 3-4).

For the Father loveth the Son, and showeth Him all things that Himself doeth: and greater works than these will He show Him, that ye may marvel. For as the Father raiseth the dead and giveth them life, even so the Son also giveth life to whom He will... For as the Father hath life in Himself, even so gave He to the Son also to have life in Himself: and He gave Him authority to execute judgment, because He is a Son of man (John 5:20-21, 26-27).

...the glory which I had with Thee before the world was (John 17:5).

There are three main directions in which spiritual sight is necessary; firstly, with regard to the place and significance of Christ in the Divine scheme of things; then, with regard to the place and significance of man in that scheme; and thirdly, concerning the reality, ways, and objective of the evil spiritual powers in this universe. These three things very largely comprehend the Scriptures. Here, we shall be mainly occupied with the first of these.

The Place and Significance of Christ

There are two sides to Christ's person and work. (1) Christ as the Son of God. (2) Christ as the Son of Man. When we have gathered up all that is said and intimated in the Scriptures about Jesus as the Son of God we are led to one comprehensive conclusion. It is this, that God's sole rights and prerogatives have been vested by Him in His Son, and God has bound Himself to be personally and definitely known only Sonwise. There is neither access nor knowledge of a personal nature, nor fellowship, apart from the Son. "No man cometh to the Father, but by Me" (John 14:6). "No one knoweth the Father save the Son, and he to whomsoever the Son willeth to reveal Him" (Matt. 11:27). That revelation is in the Son alone. "He that hath seen Me hath seen the Father" (John 14:9). Then we have to ask, What are those unique and sole rights of God which are vested in the Son?

The First is:

The Prerogative of Life

When we really come to deal with life, we come to deal with God. While there is something of life present man may have a place. He may help, stimulate, feed, and co-operate with it; but when life has departed, man has no more place and it is God's matter alone. Only

God can deal with that situation. The question of life from the dead is God's matter alone. For a whole generation this question raged as a battle, and very largely it raged around one man - Louis Pasteur. During the whole of his life-time the question of spontaneous generation flamed and fumed and divided men into schools of fierce antagonism. But before he died the question was settled and today no knowledgeable person believes otherwise than that life only comes from life, and never from death - that is, in the realm of nature. Thus the field is left clear for the supernatural, and life out of death is God's unique sphere. What is true in the natural is also true in the spiritual. The life which we all have in common as the life of soul and body is one thing, and the above law holds good with regard to it. But there is another life; it is uncreated life, Divine life, what we call spiritual life. That is another thing altogether. A hundred or more people may be here together, all of them alive in the first sense, but only a few may be alive in the second sense. The majority, while very active in the life of soul and body, may be quite dead with regard to uncreated, Divine life. Thus are people divided, and in this way they are two entirely different orders of creation, species of beings.

Much has been said and written about the immortality of the soul. The Bible does not teach this. Continuity and immortality are two distinct things. Immortality is a Divine prerogative and feature. "Who only hath immortality" (1 Tim. 6:16). Immortality is that Divine nature which is characteristic of Divine life. It is something altogether higher than just survival of physical disintegration and the grave. This latter without immortality or immortal life must be a very horrible thing. It is what the Bible means - metaphorically - by being "naked" and "ashamed". So the apostle speaks of immortality as being "clothed upon", that "mortality may be swallowed up of life."

Thus the giving of that life is with God alone, and those who have it are thereby different in an inward reality from all others. They possess the basis of a complete transformation, which is the meaning of being "glorified".

But our particular message is that God has vested this life in His Son Jesus Christ, and that it cannot be had apart from Him. "As the Father hath life in Himself, even so gave He to the Son also to have life in Himself" (John 5:26). "As the Father raiseth the dead and giveth them life, even so the Son... giveth life to whom He will" (John 5:21). The gospel of the glory of Christ is that God has given Him the glory of being able to give eternal life, incorruptible, immortal life to those who believe on Him. "This life is in His Son. He that hath the Son hath the life" (1 John 5:11-12). Once that life has been imparted all the glorious thoughts and purposes of God for men have been started on their way to realization. So what comes in with Christ is the life of a new creation, a new universe. Everything is to be realized on the biological principle, but it is a life which is different in nature, capacity, and consciousness from all other life. Being peculiarly God's own Divine life it is the basis and link of true inward fellowship with Him. In this way we are able to see something of the immense and vital significance of Christ.

To accept Christ in a living and positive way is to receive a life which means an inward and secret difference in our very constitution, and to be in the way of possibilities which are denied all others.

To reject or neglect Christ is to lose or miss all that God ever intended when He created man and put him on a probation of faith. Herein lies the immense peril of prevarication or procrastination. It is not in man's power to say when that life shall be offered to him. When Christ is presented, that is the time when life and death are in the balances of our acceptance or rejection, and the very greatest eternal values and issues are bound up with that decision. To all this the great enemy of men's eternal glory would blind them and keep them blind. One of the blinding lies of the Devil is the lie of evolution. While we all believe in a certain development and progress, the doctrine which declares that man started with the amoeba and in the course of many thousands - perhaps millions - of years passes through numerous stages - e.g. of ape, primitive man, civilized man, angelic being, and so on - and finally becomes a god, having attained deity! - this is a lie and a deception, and is intended by its satanic inventor to keep men from accepting Christ. For all this progress (?) is said to be made altogether without any outside intervention. Someone writing on this matter has put it in this way: We have heard of a wonderful machine which, with claws, takes hold of so much leather at one end and draws it in and, without any outside intervention, takes it through stage after stage, and pours it forth as shoes at the other end: without any outside intervention! And, says the writer, that is evolution; the claws take hold on the amoeba and draw it in, and then evolution is supposed to take it through various stages and at last turn it out as angels and gods. But, says he, unfortunately the amoeba at a certain point gets caught in the mesh and in the end beasts come out, tearing one another to pieces! Are men really nearer angels and gods today after these thousands of years? Is the moral life of the race so much higher after all? Only the very blind will say it is.

Ah, it is just in that little clause "outside intervention" that everything is found. There will never really be any true conformity to God's likeness without outside intervention. It will not work like a machine. This outside intervention is set forth in the words of Christ: "I am come that they might have life" (John 10:10). There is no hope of man reaching God by himself, but God has intervened in the person of His Son and with Him offered the life which has in it the power to bring us into oneness with Him in likeness and fellowship.

God's Prerogative of Light Vested in the Son

The second prerogative of God is light. It was God Who said, Let there be light, light shall be! Light is with God. Of course, there are many intimations in the Scriptures of that in the natural realm. God makes darkness and light, and God, when He chooses, can break into the ordinary course of things in that matter and turn light to darkness or darkness to light. He can divide in the same territory between light and darkness; when all Egypt is in darkness, gross darkness, with the plague resting upon it, the children of Israel have light in their dwellings. Right within the same land, light and darkness simultaneously existed by a Divine intervention from the outside. Yes, light can be preserved and maintained by God beyond the due course, and darkness can be brought in prematurely when it ought to be light.

There is much in the Old Testament about that, and it is carried over into the New Testament. When the Son of God was crucified, darkness was over the face of the land until the ninth hour. Put out God's Son and you put out God's light. That is the point. Light is God's prerogative.

What is illustrated by God's dealings in nature is the great truth of spiritual light; that spiritual light is God's prerogative, that He can bring light into darkness at any given moment, He does not have to wait for a course of things: and He can shut out the light at any given moment. It is in His power to do that.

Thus this second prerogative of God, namely, that of light, is also vested in Jesus Christ, His Son, and bound up with Him. "I am the light of the world" (John 9:5). "In the beginning was the Word, and the Word was with God, and the Word was God... In Him was life; and the life was the light of men". "No man hath seen God at any time; the only begotten Son, Who is in the bosom of the Father, He hath declared Him", "He hath revealed Him" (John 1:18). It is the glory of Christ to be able, at any given moment, to break in upon our darkness, and has it not just been that which has brought His glory into our hearts and brought glory out from our hearts to Him, when by that blessed touch of His finger (the Spirit of God) we have been able to say suddenly, I see! I never saw it like that! What is then the spontaneous desire of our hearts? It is to worship Him.

We revert to that man born blind, to whom the Lord gave sight and eventually interrogated him with the inquiry, "Dost thou believe on the Son of God?" He answered and said, And who is he, Lord, that I may believe on him? Jesus said unto him, Thou hast both seen Him, and He it is that speaketh with thee. And he said, Lord, I believe. And he worshipped Him. Why did he worship? Because the Son of God for him was one thing with having his sight. The two things went together. Having his sight was bound up with this One Who could be none other than the Son of God to give thee sight. That is what the Lord meant by having that incident included in that gospel, the whole purpose of which is to give evidence that Jesus is the Son of God. You know how John concludes his gospel - If everything was written that could be written, I suppose that even the world itself would not contain the books that should be written; but these things are written, "that ye may believe that Jesus is the Christ, the Son of God' and that believing ye may have life in His name" (John 20:30). And this is written in the book which has that as its object. When the disciples say, Lord, who did sin, this man, or his parents, that he should be born blind?, the Lord Jesus dismissed that superstition by saying, "Neither did this man sin, nor his parents; but that the works of God should be made manifest in him". And the Son is the instrument of the works of God. The Lord Jesus had already said that the Father works, and the works that the Father does, the Son also does, and greater works than these will He show Him. The works of God - giving sight, through the Son, to those born blind, leading to worship; and God does not mind you worshipping His Son, He will not be jealous of His Son, because He has bound Himself up with His Son and put His Son on an equality with Himself, and vested His own rights and prerogatives in His Son. To worship the Son is to worship the Father, because the Father and the Son are one.

Well, that Jesus is the Son of God is evidenced by people getting spiritual sight, and that is the glory of Christ, to be able to do that, leading, as we were saying, to worship. It is a great thing to recognize even a little of this. It is a great thing to have our eyes opened. It is a great thing to have our eyes opened initially and foundationally; it is a great thing as we go along to have our eyes opened again and again to see what no one has been able to show us, what we have struggled to see and understand; and then God sovereignly, by intervention from outside, touches our spiritual eyes and we see. Is it not a great day when we see like that?

Some of us know what it is to have something in the Word of God. We sense there is something in that passage that we have not got; there is the Divine meaning, but we cannot get it; and we have walked round it, we have looked to see if anybody could help us. We have gone to all the authorities on that particular passage, but we have not got it. There are a lot of good things being said, but somehow we are not getting what we sense is there. We put it back to the Lord and say, Now, Lord, if you want us to have that, you show us at the right time when it is necessary, not just for the sake of information but when it is going to serve a purpose. And we have gone on and left it with the Lord, and going on quietly, perhaps occupied with something else, the whole thing has just come up and been broken upon us, and we have seen it, and our faces have become wreathed with smiles. We can put our finger upon many things like that in the course of our life. They have just come and we have received them. You cannot take that away from us.

Now my point here is simply to illustrate what a tremendous thing this breaking in of light upon us is, how it lifts us out, how it fills us with glory, how it changes the outlook when there breaks in spiritual light, light which never was on land or sea, light from above. And the Lord Jesus is the sum of that Divine light. He is the light. If only our eyes were opened to see the significance of the Lord Jesus, what a tremendous difference it would make, how we should be emancipated. The need is that, to see the Son of God as having vested in Him the prerogative of Divine light-giving, because He is the light. It is with Him to come right into our scene of darkness and drive the darkness out. That is His glory, and you can know the glory of the Son of God, you can worship Him, because your eyes are opened.

He is here. Just as He, being the resurrection and the life, means resurrection at any moment, and not merely at the last day - you remember Martha said, "I know that he shall rise again in the resurrection at the last day", and the Lord, in effect, said, Stop, I am the resurrection and the life, and I being here, the last day may be here so far, as the resurrection is concerned; it is no time matter when I am present, it can be now! - So He, being here, there may be a new creation now with a new creation light: not, I shall get light later on, but now; by this glorious intervention from without.

The glory of Jesus Christ which He had with the Father before the world was, the glory of the Son is that; that He has this sole Divine prerogative, right, power and ability to bring light. No one else can give it; it is not possible to attain unto that light. It is His gift, it is His act. That is His glory.

God's Prerogative of Lordship Vested in the Son

One final word with reference to the glory of Jesus Christ as God's Son. The Divine prerogative of government is vested in Him. The third prerogative of God is government. In the last issue, the decision is with God in all matters. Over and above all things, God is: He rules, and He rules in the kingdoms of men and among the armies of heaven. He governs, but He has now vested that government in His Son. "Neither doth the Father judge any man, but He hath given all judgment unto the Son" (John 5:22). This Divine prerogative of government, therefore, is vested in Christ.

What does that mean for us now? "The gospel of the glory of Christ." "We preach Christ Jesus as Lord". That is in substance one statement - the glory of Christ, Christ Jesus as Lord. I think I must leave a great deal of the detail and leap right to the end of that. The glory of Christ is only recognized when He is Lord, but it is recognized when He is Lord. I mean that God is satisfied when His Son comes unto the appointed place, and God can never be satisfied in any one direction without the one affected being aware of it.

There is always an echo here of something in the heart of God which affects us. I mean that if heaven rejoices over one sinner that repenteth, that sinner will never fail to have the echo of heaven's joy. The joy which comes to a repentant sinner is not just his own joy, it is the joy of heaven, it has come of what is going on above. When the Father is well-pleased, it will be witnessed in the one in whom He is well-pleased. "This is My beloved Son, in Whom I am well pleased" (Matt. 3:17). The Son knows in His own spirit, His own heart, the delight of the Father. "The Father loveth the Son": He can say that without any conceit or presumption: and when the place to which the Son has been assigned by the Father is given to the Son in any life, or in any company, or in any place on this earth, then you may take it that the heaven is opened there, and the Father's gratification will be registered there. You never get through a struggle and battle on some question of His Lordship without knowing a new Divine joy and peace and rest in your heart. A struggle has been going on over a matter of obedience to something in the will of God, something the Lord has said: there has been a battle over it for a long time and at last you get through - "My stubborn will at last hath yielded" - and you are through. The Lord's Lordship is established, and what is the result? Rest, peace, joy, satisfaction. You say, What a fool I was to keep that up for so long. What is it? It is not just a psychological relief, that you have got past a difficult place: it is the Spirit of God bearing witness within. It is the Holy Dove lighting upon your spirit. It is the Father's good pleasure witnessed to in your heart, the Lordship of God in Christ established. We can never in reality believe in the absolute Lordship of God and not give Christ His place. That is a contradiction. For the Lordship of God to be a reality, Christ has to be Lord in our hearts. We need to see that.

The Practical Issue

What I really want to leave with you in this last word is this: do pray for the Lord to open your eyes to the meaning of the Lordship of Christ. You know, beloved, all our troubles circle round that issue. Other lords have had dominion over us. What are those other lords? There are lords many. Our own souls may be having dominion, our own sentimentalities, our own likes and preferences and judgments, our own dislikes and antipathies, our own traditions, our own teachers: these may be governing us. Oh, the lords are so many, and they may just be governing. The Lord is desirous of bringing us into a larger and freer place, and a place of an opened heaven: something is still tyrannizing: we are in the center, the natural self-life is on the throne, we have a horrible way of drawing everything to ourselves. Immediately anything is raised, we step into the center of the arena, the self-life ruling on the throne: and what kind of life is it? Well, it is a life of shadows, to say the least of it; it is a life of limitation, of variableness, up and down, of weakness and uncertainty. If we want to come right out into the light, the full light, to go right on in the full light, in the glorious liberty of the children of God, all those other lords have to be deposed, and Christ has to be Lord.

Now, while I am saying that, you agree with me absolutely. You say, Yes, of course we want Christ to be Lord, we want nothing more than that Christ should be Lord, and we know He has to be Lord: we know that God has made Him both Lord and Christ! We assent. Beloved, that is all right, but what about it? When we have assented, when we have agreed, are we still going to assert our own judgments, are we still going to meet others and things in our own strength? Are we still going to be in the picture, are we still going to allow those old dominations to influence us? This establishment of Christ as Lord is a thing which can only be done, not by assent, not by agreement, although that may be required: - it can only be done by our being broken down, and we have to say to the Lord, Lord, you break down everything that You find in the way: take in hand whatever there is that obstructs Your absolute Lordship.

"The dearest idol I Have known, Whate'er that idol be, Help me to tear it from Thy Throne And worship only Thee".

There may be something very dear, a part of our very being, and it is in the way: our very life, our very self. There is something to be done right in us, but oh, that we should see how much hangs upon the place and significance of Christ in the Divine economy of things, Christ as Lord. What hangs upon that? It is the glory of Christ.

Have you ever got through to a new position with the Lord where His Lordship has been established in some new way, in some new matter, in some new sphere? Have you ever got through and been miserable about it, felt you have lost everything? You know to the contrary. The experience may have been a very deep and terrible one, but when you are through, you glorify God. When the Lord is dealing with things that are in the way of His Lordship, it is a dark time, full of suffering, but you are going to come to the place where you thank God for every bit of it. How can that be? If the Lord should make windows in heavens, might this thing be? That is what we feel when we are in the process, but I am certain, and experience in some degree bears it out, that when we are on the other side of that and the Lord has a new place in our lives, we thank Him for the depths, and we say, You were right, faithful and true. You can say that as a bit of your faith, but it is a great thing to say it as a bit of your experience. Faithful and true!

The glory of God in the face of Jesus Christ, the glory of Christ, the gospel of the glory of Christ as son of God is all brought to us in terms of Life and Light and Lordship - the three L's of the glory of God's Son. The Lord lead us into that.

Chapter 11

Seeing the Glory of Christ as Son of Man

God, having of old time spoken unto the fathers in the prophets by divers portions and in divers manners, hath at the end of these days spoken unto us in His Son, Whom He appointed Heir of all things, through Whom also He made the worlds (Heb. 1:1-2; A.R.V.).

For not unto angels did He subject the world to come, whereof we speak. But one hath somewhere testified, saying, 'What is man, that Thou art mindful of him? Or the Son of Man, that Thou visitest Him? Thou madest Him a little lower than the angels; Thou crowned Him with glory and honor, and didst set Him over the works of Thy hands: Thou didst put all things in subjection under His feet.' For in that He subjected all things unto Him, He left nothing that is not subject to Him. But now we see not yet all things subjected to Him. But we behold Him Who hath been made a little lower than the angels, even Jesus, because of the suffering of death crowned with glory and honor, that by the grace of God He should taste of death for every man. For it became Him, for Whom are all things, and through Whom are all things, in bringing many sons unto glory, to make the Author of their salvation perfect through sufferings. For both He that sanctifieth and they that are sanctified are all of One: for which cause He is not ashamed to call them brethren, saying, 'I will declare Thy Name unto My brethren, in the midst of the congregation will I sing Thy praise.' And again, 'I will put My trust in Him.' And again, 'Behold, I and the children whom God hath given Me.' Since then the children are sharers in flesh and blood, He also Himself in like manner partook of the same; that through death He might bring to naught him that had the power of death, that is, the devil; and might deliver all them who through fear of death were all their lifetime subject to bondage. For verily not to angels doth He give help, but He giveth help to the seed of Abraham. Wherefore it behooved Him in all things to be made like unto His brethren, that He might become a merciful and faithful high priest in things pertaining to God, to make propitiation for the sins of the people. For in that He Himself hath suffered being tempted, He is able to succor them that are tempted (Heb. 2:5-18).

Wherefore, holy brethren, partakers of a heavenly calling, consider the Apostle and High Priest of our confession, even Jesus (Heb. 3:1).

In whom the god of this world hath blinded the minds of the unbelieving, that the light of the gospel of the glory of Christ, Who is the image of God, should not dawn upon them. For we preach not ourselves, but Christ Jesus as Lord, and ourselves as your servants for Jesus' sake (2 Cor. 4:4-5).

In our previous meditation we were seeing the glory and significance of Christ as the Son of God, having vested in Him the prerogatives of God; firstly, the power of Life; secondly, the power of Light; and thirdly, the power of Lordship.

In this meditation we shall spend our time with another aspect of the glory of Christ, namely, the glory and peculiar significance of Christ as Son of Man. It is here also that we need spiritual sight. If men could really see from God's standpoint, with God's own knowledge and understanding, the Lord Jesus Christ as Son of Man, all the problems of this world would be solved: for really there is a sense in which all problems are solved when we see. And God's solution is His Son. Let us be found here this afternoon in our hearts waiting on the Lord that we might see. Let that be our attitude: to see Jesus in an inward way with the eyes of the heart enlightened, the

Spirit of wisdom and revelation being given us in the knowledge of Him.

If I might say so here, I feel that the burden of our hearts should be that the eyes of the Lord's people should be opened first. Oh, if only their eyes were open, what different attitudes they would take, what great possibilities there would be for God, what a lot of things would disappear which are dishonoring to the Lord! If only they could see! Let us pray much that the eyes of the people of God may be opened. And then, to the end that the eyes of men at large might be opened, let us pray that there might be an eye-opening ministry like that of Paul - "...unto whom I send thee, to open their eyes, that they may turn from darkness to light" (Acts. 26:17-18). Let us pray along such lines continually.

The Arch-Type of a New Humanity

I think there are two or three particular aspects of Christ as Son of Man. Firstly, this is the human title of Christ, and it brings to us at once the conception of Him as man, or as humanity, and the thing needed to be seen about the Lord Jesus is the Divine meaning in His humanity. As Son of Man it is not only that He has come alongside of us, taking flesh and blood, and so becoming a man, and just being here as a man among men. Oh no, that is not it. True He is man, true He has become partaker of flesh and blood, but there is a difference, a vast and infinite difference. Humanity, yes; but not exactly our humanity. The significance of Christ as Son of Man is that He is an arch-type of a new humanity.

There are now in God's universe two humanities, whereas there was only one. The Adam humanity was the only one, but there is Another Humanity now, a different humanity; flesh and bone, but without the sinful nature of this humanity, without any of that which has estranged and alienated this humanity from God, without any of that which brought this humanity under judgment from God, a humanity upon which God, in His infinite holiness and perfection, can look with pleasure and utter satisfaction. "My beloved Son in Whom I am well-pleased"? (Matt. 3:17). It is a Man, but such a man as is not common among men, but altogether different. The significance of Christ as Son of Man is that God has started a new humanity according to His own mind and perfect thought, and in His Son there is the arch-type of that new humanity to which God is going to conform a race - "conformed to the image of His Son" (Rom. 8:29).

The great reality about a true Christian is that he or she is progressively being changed into another, is becoming different. It is not just and only an objective matter of faith in Christ as outward. It is more than that; it is living by Christ inwardly.

So God has come into this realm of humanity in the Person of His Son as representing a new order altogether, a new order of mankind, and, by vital union with Christ, a new race is springing up, a new order. A new kind of humanity is secretly growing, and proceeding unto that day of which the Apostle speaks, when there will be the manifestation of the sons of God; and then the curse will be lifted, and the creation itself will be delivered from the bondage of corruption into the liberty of the glory of the children of God.

Now the point is the tremendous significance of the Incarnation, of the Word becoming flesh and tabernacling among us, the tremendous significance of Christ as Son of Man, as setting up amongst men a new kind of being, a new type and form of humanity. There is no hope for the creation save in that new type, that new order. If men saw this, would it not solve all the problems of this time? What are they talking about? What is the great phrase most common on men's lips today? Is it not a new order, a new world order? But they are blind, they talk in the dark: they are groping for something, but they see not. The only new order is the order of the Son of Man. The only hope for this world is that there shall come about this new creation in Christ Jesus.

The Truth Foreshadowed in Israel's History

We could dwell long upon the humanity of the Lord Jesus. There is a very great deal more in the Scripture about it than perhaps you realize. But do notice that God has laid this deep in the very foundations of history. You take Israel as God's great object lesson for past ages - and their history of the past still stands as the great book of illustrations of God's principles - and you find that the very national life of Israel of old was founded upon those things which set forth the perfect humanity of the Lord Jesus.

You go to the Book of Leviticus, and you take up those feasts: you see what a place the humanity (the fine flour) has in those symbols and types. You see that God has said there in illustration that the life of a people which is to satisfy Him is based upon a nature, a humanity: not the old broken-down humanity of Adam, but another. Right into the very foundation of the life of such a people, there is laid this reality: there is a humanity that is perfect and incorruptible: and out from those feasts must be extricated every suggestion and suspicion of leaven, which speaks of corruption, the ferment of the old nature. It has no place when it is a matter of the very basis of Israel's life God-ward.

Well, you see, there is much about it, but we are not going to explore the whole ground. I simply want to point out the fact that the humanity of the Lord Jesus as Son of Man sets forth some new kind, some new type, some new order, in God's universe which does satisfy God.

Herein lies the tremendous and wonderful meaning of union with Christ through faith, bringing us right into what He is in His acceptability to God. The practical outworking of that must be that you and I - more and more - forsake the ground of the old Adam, of nature, our ground, and abide in Christ. That just means holding by faith to what He is and letting go what we are, and so the pleasure of God is found there. If we get on to our own ground, what we are by nature, and take account of that and try to make something good of that, or even spend our time deploring what a miserable thing that nature is, we lose all the glory of God. The glory of God is in another humanity. Dwell on Christ, abide in Christ, and the glory is there. It is the glory of Christ as the Son of Man. What are the most blessed and glorious hours in the Christian's experience? Are they not the hours in which they are contemplating and taken up with what Christ is?

The Redeemer-Kinsman

Then the glory of Christ as Son of Man is to be seen in Him as the Redeemer-Kinsman. Firstly, as the arch-type of a new humanity; then, secondly, as the Redeemer-Kinsman. Your thoughts will at once go to that little classic, the Book of Ruth. I need not tell you the story of Ruth in detail, but it is from there that we draw the great truths and principles of the redeeming activity of the Lord.

The story in brief is this. The inheritance has been lost. The day comes when that inheritance becomes a matter of solemn, sad, but earnest concern to the hearts of those who have lost it. Now the realization has come home to them that the inheritance has passed out of their control and right; and they are deeply exercised in heart about the lost inheritance. There is only one way, according to the law of things, in which that lost inheritance can be re-purchased, and that is that there should be a kinsman - he must be a kinsman, he must be of their own kin - who has the right to redeem, and who has the ability to redeem, and who is willing to redeem. Those who lost the inheritance, and have now become so deeply concerned about its recovery, are looking for that redeemer-kinsman who has the right, who has the ability, the resource, and who has the willingness to redeem the lost inheritance. You know how Ruth comes into touch with Boaz, and thinking him to be the redeemer-kinsman, recognizing that if he has the will, he has the resource, she discovers that he has not the right, because there is another who comes first. An appeal has to be made to the one who has the right, and it is found that, while he has the right, he has neither ability nor resource: and he passes over his right to Boaz. Thus at length the one wholly fitted for the business is found in Boaz. He has now the right, he has the resource and the ability, and he has the will to do it.

But then there is one other thing in the story. According to the law of things, the redeemer-kinsman has to take to wife the one for whom he redeems the inheritance, and the way has got to be cleared for that. The other kinsman could not do it because the way was not clear for that, but Boaz has a clear way to do it.

There are the elements of the story. I am not going to take up every little detail, but just the broad outline. You see how God has placed there such an exquisite illustration of the glory of Christ as the Redeemer-Kinsman. The inheritance has been lost, and all that God intended for man has been forfeited. Man now, through Adam's sin, has lost the inheritance. In Adam, no longer is he heir of all things, the inheritance is gone. The tragedy of this humanity in Adam is just that: once an heir, made to inherit, but now bankrupt, hopeless, having lost all. That is the tragedy of this humanity. That is where we are by nature. We have it written in our beings. Our very nature witnesses to the fact that there is something lacking, something missing, something that ought to be and is not. We are groping for it. It is in the very nature of things to crave, to long for that. Every ambition of man, every quest, every passion of man, is man shouting out of his nature that there is something he ought to have but cannot get. He accumulates all that this world can give him, and dies, saying, No, I have not got it, I have not found what I am after! He is an heir with a lost inheritance.

The Right to Redeem

And into a world like that, into a race like that, God, in His Son, in terms of manhood, comes from the outside as the Redeemer-Kinsman. He has, first of all, the right to redeem. Why? Because He is the Firstborn of all creation. He has the First Place. This is no second-place kinsman. "He is before all things" (Col. 1:17). He is the Firstborn; He has the right because of place, the place He occupies, the First Place. Oh, think again of all that there is about the Lord Jesus as coming first, as being in the First Place, as being the Firstborn, and you will see that constitutes His right, for in the very nature of things in the Bible, it is the Firstborn, who carries the rights with him always. Here is Jesus, Son of Man, the first by appointment and placing of God. He has the right to redeem.

The Power to Redeem

He has also the power to redeem, that is, He has the resources for redeeming. Well, let us ask what is in the nature of things required for redeeming? The inheritance has to be redeemed not only for us but unto God. We in turn are God's inheritance, we are God's possession by right, and not only have we lost our inheritance, but God has lost His inheritance in us, and what we might be satisfied with as a return, God can never be satisfied with. If God is to get back in us that inheritance which He Himself has lost through man's sin and willfulness, its redemption must be according to God, something that satisfies God: and God cannot be satisfied with just anything. It must be something that wholly answers to God's own nature. So let us say at once that "we were redeemed, not with corruptible things, with silver or gold, from our vain manner of life... but with precious blood, as of a Lamb without blemish" (1 Pet. 1:18-19). What is it that satisfies God? It is an incorruptible something. That which can alone bring back to God His satisfaction must be incorruptible, undefiled, without spot or blemish. These are words which always relate to Christ: a Lamb, without spot, without blemish. That is the redemption resource, the redemption power. Redemption means to recover the lost inheritance, and He has redeemed by His Blood, because that Blood represents His life which is an incorruptible life, a sinless life, a life which wholly satisfies an utterly righteous and holy God. That is the price of redemption. Oh, to see the humanity of the Lord Jesus in its incorruptibility, is to see the mighty power to redeem. Set aside the Lord Jesus and you set aside the whole power of redemption, the whole right of redemption; there is no hope of redemption. We can never be redeemed unto God with such corruptible things as silver and gold. To be redeemed unto God means that a life must be forthcoming which is according to God's own nature.

Oh, this is where all the blindness is. We spoke in our previous meditation of the terrible blindness which is seen in evolution. But here is the awful blindness of that terrible gospel, which is not a gospel at all, which is being preached, namely, humanism; that it is in man's own power to become like God. The roots and seeds of perfection are deep down in man's own being if only he will dig deep enough for them; there is no need for intervention from the outside at all; it is not necessary for God to intervene, for Christ to come into this world. It is in man to rise, he can improve himself. He is a wonderful creature deep down in his being. What blindness! You say, Amazing thing in the light of present happenings and present world conditions; amazing thing that any man can believe it, let alone preach it; amazing thing that with one breath they talk about the awful atrocities which are worse than those of the dark ages, and with the next breath they say it is in man to be godlike! Blindness! The real point is this: are men more noble morally today? Are men morally rising? Well, who can say "Yes!" in the light of what we know today.

And yet they are preaching this gospel of humanism, that man is steadily rising and Utopia is on the horizon; because man has it in himself to rise! That is blindness, terrible blindness. But oh! To see God's Son, the Son of Man, is to see the hope, the direction in which redemption lies; because redemption lies in the direction of another kind of humanity, and in a power to redeem, because there is something there which satisfies God, and anything which does not satisfy God can never be a redeeming power. Has the Lord Jesus the power? We here all cry with one voice, Yes, He has the power, He has the resource for doing this.

The Liberty to Redeem

But another question arises. Is He free to redeem? One thing is taken for granted in this matter of the redeeming kinsman, and that is that he can only have one wife. If he is already married he is disqualified, because he cannot marry the person for whom he redeems the inheritance. That was the trouble with the other kinsman, in the case of Ruth. He was not free; he was married and had a family. But Boaz was unmarried, was free, and he could take Ruth to wife; the way was perfectly clear.

Now we come into the realm of sublime things spiritually. "Christ loved the church and gave Himself for it, that He might redeem it from all iniquity" (Eph. 5:25; Titus 2:14). "Husbands, love your wives, even as Christ also loved the church, and gave Himself up for it." The redeemed is to be joined to the Lord, and the Lord Jesus - may I say it reverently? - is only going to have one wife. There is only going to be one marriage supper of the Lamb. The Church is His only Bride. His redeemed are the only ones to be brought into such a relationship with Himself; and the way is clear. He stands perfectly free to redeem, and to take the consequences of redeeming, even of marrying the one for whom the inheritance is redeemed.

Does not redemption bring us into a very sacred position with the Lord Jesus? That is the true significance of the title that attaches to Him as our Redeemer-Kinsman, that we should be joined to Him. Not redeemed as a chattel, not redeemed as a thing, but redeemed to be joined to Him forever in the holiest of all bonds. Married to the Lord. That is the meaning of the Son of Man. Yes, He is free, He can do it.

The Willingness to Redeem

Only one question remains. Is He willing? He has the right, He has the resource, He has the liberty. Will He? Oh, how Ruth and Naomi must have waited with bated breath and thumping hearts while that final question was being met and answered. Will he? Ah, but there may be no thumping heart here this today, no bated breath. Will He? Is He willing? Well, what do we say to that? He has done it, and that answers the question. All that remains, if we are not in the enjoyment of it, is for us to accept it, believe it. He is willing!

May the Lord just ravish our hearts and enlarge our seeing of Jesus, the Son of Man.

Part III

Spiritual Hearing

Chapter 12

The Ear for the Lord Alone

Reading: Rom. 12:1; Ex. 21:5-6; Deut. 15:12-18; Lev. 8:22-24,30; 14:28; Isa. 1:4-5; Rev. 3:20-22.

You will have noticed that, in all these passages, reference is made to the ear. There is the bored ear of the servant, the consecrated ear of the priest, the anointed ear of the leper, the opened ear for instruction in Isa. 1, and the attentive ear of Rev. 3. It is impressive to realize what a large place the Lord gives to the ear and how much Scripture is occupied with hearing; and, as we put the various Scriptures together, we come to find that the matter of hearing, or of the ear, goes right to the root of the spiritual life. It was by capturing the ear of Eve that all sin was introduced into the human race. She consented to listen, she lent her ear when the adversary, Satan, said, "Hath God said...?". That was the beginning of all spiritual evil among men, and since then Satan has ever sought to propagate his kingdom by getting the ear, by securing a consent to listen. It was in exactly the same way that he went to the Lord Jesus in the days of His fast in the wilderness, saying, "If thou be the Son of God..." There is something in that very much akin to "Hath God said...?", because it was only a short time previously that God had said, "This is my beloved Son". But the last Adam (Christ) refused to listen; He closed His ear. He would not consent to entertain the suggestion and by His persistent refusal to give ear to the adversary, redemption was accomplished. All the mischief of the first failure in that very respect was overcome.

When we come to the book of the Revelation, we find that it is to the ear that the appeal is made. It is the time of consummations. The first chapters have to do with things that must be listened to as from the Lord; the last chapters see the result of that work of the Spirit-life in fullness; the same principles as in Genesis. It is the question of life in fullness, lost by lending an ear to Satan, gained by listening to what the Spirit saith.

So we are right in saying that there is a sense in which the whole spiritual life and spiritual history hang upon spiritual hearing. Between the two extremes of death and life, between listening to Satan and having an ear only for the Lord, there are many aspects of spiritual hearing, as we have seen in the above passages. We will not touch upon them now in detail, but be content for the moment to emphasize the necessity of having an ear to hear what the Spirit saith, and of using it - "He that hath an ear, let him hear". We must be sure that we are not only hearing outwardly, but that the thing is going deep inside, that it is making a difference. You can say things again and again to some people, and they know what you say, and will retort, 'I have heard you say that before'. But it makes no difference - they have not heard with the inward ear. Life depends upon that kind of hearing inside - using the ear that we have for what the Spirit saith. So it is all summed up in *"I beseech you therefore, brethren, by the mercies of God, to present your bodies a living sacrifice, holy, acceptable to God, which is your spiritual service (worship, R.V.M)" (Rom. 12:1).*

Chapter 13

The Pierced Ear of the Servant

Reading: Ex. 21:5-6; Deut. 15:12-18.

Here we have the ear of the servant, and right on the surface there lies the connection between love, the ear, and abiding service. Love here is connected with the bored ear, and becomes the basis of this continuous service which is something that is voluntarily entered into and cannot be legally imposed. It is something which is taken up by the servant because of a heart attitude and a heart relationship. The love basis leads to the resigning of certain rights and liberties. This servant has the right to go free. He is not a foreigner, he is not a hireling who, under compulsion, is put to bond-service. He is a Hebrew, and as such he has rights, and his rights are in the realm of liberty. He may go out free without violating any law or obligation. Indeed, it is his master who is under obligation to him at the time. But this servant resigns his rights and his liberties because of love. It is something other than constraint by legal obligation. It brings into another realm altogether.

Paul himself, who so often referred to himself as the bondservant of Jesus Christ, in various statements indicates something of the meaning of this resigning of liberties. For instance, he says, *"All things are lawful for me, but not all things are expedient" (1 Cor. 6:12).* 'I have rights, if I followed the line of rights. There is nothing to forbid me or to compel me so far as law is concerned, but I am actuated by something more than that; there are other considerations; the Lord's interests and my concern for Him lead me to forego certain liberties and rights; I resign them voluntarily for His sake.' It is the bond-slave recognizing that, while there may be nothing against certain things as judged by the ordinary standards of right and wrong, and that certain courses are quite permissible, yet some higher interest may come where the Lord can be better and more fully served if even those liberties are resigned for His sake. It is a much higher level, this level of the servant who says, 'I will not go out free; I might, I have perfect right to do so, but I will not. I am not here simply because I must be or because I am compelled - I am here out of love'. That is a fuller and a higher world altogether and it may touch us at many points. We could... we might... there would be no wrong... but the Lord's highest interests require that we should on some things deny ourselves and say, 'Though there is no wrong, no harm, the Lord will be better served if I do not'. That is what is here. "All things are lawful... but not all things are expedient"; and when that attitude is taken, a new relationship with the Lord is set up, a relationship of service in perpetuity; but now it is more as one of the household, one of the family. The Spirit of Sonship enters in, and "thou art no longer a bond-servant but, a son" (Gal. 4:7). Love lifts and transfers, and, although it is still service, we find a remarkable relatedness in the New Testament, between the bond-slave and, at the same time, the son.

We find that the Lord Jesus becomes the great example. He had rights, very great rights: He could have held to them. He had liberties: He could have stood for them. There was no obligation upon Him legally to do anything but to remain in the eternal glory with the Father. He surrendered all His rights and His liberties. He took upon Himself "the form of a servant (bond-servant)... becoming obedient even unto death, yea, the death of the cross" (Phil. 2:7-8). He said "I will not go out free"; and the Father bored His ear. He is the eternal Son-Servant. In Him the two combine - sonship and servanthood are bound together in love for the Father. And what is in its highest and fullest expression in Him is transferred to us in our smaller way. Love requires sometimes that we have to say 'No' to some things which in themselves are harmless, and, in a way, desirable, and which would be quite permissible if we were serving only our own interests. To them we say 'No' in the interests of the One Whom has become to us more than Master; He has become Lord.

Chapter 14

The Consecrated Ear

Reading: Lev. 8:22-24,30; 14:25-28.

The Blood Touched Ear

In the former of these two passages we read of the consecration of Aaron and his sons, and the placing of the blood upon the tip of their right ears - the ear consecrated by means of the blood. The blood, as you know, was always the means of discrimination and separation; all that upon which the blood was sprinkled was separated unto the Lord, consecrated to Him. The blood - speaking of an end made to a whole regime, and provision made for an entirely new order of things - the blood stood between. You hardly need me to illustrate that from Scripture, for there is so much. Perhaps the outstanding Old Testament illustration would be the blood of the Lamb sprinkled on the door posts and the lintel of the homes of the Hebrews in Egypt. By that sprinkled blood they were marked out as separate from the Egyptians, and as a people with an entirely new future, a new history. The blood separated and the blood laid the foundation for something altogether new - from that passover they were constituted God's people in a new way. That is the principle of the blood, that it separates from one system and makes a way for another.

Now here, in the priesthood, we have that very strongly emphasized. There was the blood of the ram of consecration, and placed upon the ear, it meant quite simply that the blood was going to challenge, test and judge every presentation to the mind through the ear. The blood would interrogate everything coming to the inner life through the ear, as to where it came from, as to the nature of it. The blood would judge it and say, 'That is not of God; that is not according to the mind of the Lord; that belongs to the old creation which is in alliance with sin; that springs from the original source where Satan spoke into the ear.' The blood thus would judge everything, condemning what was not of God, and keeping the way open for the Lord - a very simple lesson, but a very powerful one. The Lord Jesus said, "Take heed what ye hear" (Mark 4:24). Priesthood here means the spiritual man, the man who is wholly unto the Lord, completely at the Lord's disposal; and the spiritual man is going to be very careful what he allows himself to hear, what he allows to enter into his mind, into his inner life, and become a part of him inwardly through his ear. He is not going to listen to everything. He is going to judge what he hears and to refuse quite a lot.

Now that may apply to a large number of things which it would be unwise to try to catalogue. We can do unspeakable damage to our own spiritual life, and make it impossible for the Lord to speak to us, if we allow ourselves to listen to that which is not of the Lord, that which is contrary to Him. The enemy has gained great power for his kingdom through the ear of the world; he has a great hold on men along the line of hearing. He uses many things - it may be certain types of music, or ways of speaking. The consecrated servant of the Lord does not allow that sort of thing voluntarily. We are in this world, and we cannot avoid hearing many things that we should not wish to hear; but the important matter is not the sounds around us that strike upon our outward ear, but our reaction thereto, whether we consent to what we hear. Do we judge it and inwardly revolt against it and refuse it, or do we lend an ear to it?

I think this may specially apply to what we allow ourselves to hear about people. Untold damage is done by gossip and by criticism. Now, there is no point in having lips to talk if there are no ears to hear, and sometimes the sealing of unwise and uncontrolled lips may come by a refusal to listen. The priest is called upon to refuse to listen to a whole realm of things, to judge it and say, 'I do not want to hear that; I am not listening to it, I am not accepting it.' You can, I am sure, see what a terrible lot of mischief exists today even amongst real children of God, caused by rumors, by talk, by passing on reports, by interpretations given to things; and how susceptible we are to that sort of thing! Well, this blood-touched ear, the consecrated ear, conveys a fundamental lesson. On the one side, it refuses to accept and to allow to pass into the inner life a whole world of things.

The Spirit-Anointed Ear

Then there is the other side - the oil-anointed ear. Both sides are seen in the case of the cleansed leper in Lev. 14. In type he is the man who is freed from the defiling life of the flesh and is walking by the Spirit, in newness of life. He has the blood-touched ear - the token of his refusal to listen to what is not of God; and he has the oil-touched ear - the token of his readiness to hearken to the Lord. What a lot is lost because so many of the Lord's people have not an ear to listen to Him - the open, sensitive, alive ear quickened by the Holy Spirit, the quiet ear. The enemy has made many of the Lord's servants too busy to stop to listen to the Lord. Things are all unsatisfactory, they are all going wrong and missing the mark; and the enemy is just carrying the workers on by the sheer momentum of the work. He is seeing to it that they have no time to hear what the Lord would say about things. Those churches at the beginning of the book of the Revelation had many commendable things, and perhaps the greatest surprise that ever came to anybody came to some of them when it was said to them, in effect, 'You have all this work, labor, patience and all these other quite commendable things, but you have not an ear to hear the Lord. These other things are not wrong, but there are very much more important things, and you are not hearing what the Spirit is saying. He that hath an ear, let him hear what the Spirit saith...' The need was for an ear open to the Lord for correction, for adjustment, for knowing His mind more fully.

There is the ear sealed against one world, and there is the ear open to the other world. There is one world closed by the Blood, another world opened by the Spirit; and it all centers in the inner ear, the ear of the heart. It is a very important thing. The Lord give us grace to be very obedient and watchful over this matter, taking heed what we hear, what we allow ourselves to receive, and keeping in that place where, if the Lord is wanting to say something, He has our ear not pre-occupied but alive to listen to His voice.

Chapter 15

The Opened Ear

Reading: Isaiah 50:4-9

This passage in Isa. 50 needs to be read closely in connection with chapter 49, and indeed recognized as to its setting in the whole of the section of the prophecies. The position is that of Israel's rebelliously going backward in spite of all the Lord's speaking to them through His prophets. They refused to open their ear to the Lord. The result? - they were, as this chapter puts it at the beginning, divorced from the Lord. They were cut off and committed to captivity; and then in these chapters up to 53, the Servant of the Lord in His redemptive work is so fully and wonderfully brought into view, and it is concerning Him that these words are spoken. They give to us some little suggestion of how the people are served unto their salvation. We have, first, sin and its consequences, and then the Redeemer-Servant and the cost of redemption. *"I gave my back to the smiters, and my cheeks to them that plucked off the hair, I hid not my face from shame and spitting"* - words which were literally fulfilled in the case of the Lord Jesus. Then His vindication is referred to in verses 7-9. *"The Lord Jehovah will help me; therefore have I not been confounded: therefore have I set my face like a flint, and I know that I shall not be put to shame. He is near that justifieth me; who will contend with me..."* and so on. It is the Lord Himself speaking in the presence of His Cross, and looking with confidence to the issue of His sufferings, His vindication in resurrection; and because of all that - the confidence that He had in God, and His willingness to pay the price of their salvation - He brings this word of hope: *"The Lord God hath given me the tongue of them that are taught, that I may know how to sustain with words him that is weary."* That is the word of hope to a people without hope in a very desperate situation, *"to sustain with words him that is weary"* - a ministry of hope through the Cross in the resurrection, in the vindication, of the suffering Servant.

Then He simply indicates the ministry of hope, of re-assurance, the word of life and salvation, that changing of the darkness to light, that it is because of the opposite attitude on His part to that which brought about the darkness and the death. They turned back rebelliously and closed their ear to the word of the Lord. He turned toward God obediently and opened His ear; that is, He listened, He took note, He received the word of the Lord. Pre-eminently this applies to the Lord Jesus, but in principle it applies to us, and the whole thing is now brought to rest upon this - a daily life governed by an ear opened to the Lord. *"He wakeneth morning by morning, he wakeneth mine ear to hear as they that are taught."* It is rather remarkable that the Lord Jesus should be saying that He is as a disciple, as a learner, as one who is taught. It shows how completely, while being of God and the Creator of all things, He is in flesh dependent utterly upon God for everything, receiving from the Father His daily direction and instruction. What a picture of self-emptying! How fully His words were true - *"The Son can do nothing of himself, but what he seeth the Father doing"* (John 5:19) - a daily dependence upon the Father for everything, and a receiving of everything from the Father. Well, of course, we know how true that is of ourselves, but it is very wonderful that His ministry of hope depended upon, and sprang out of, His waiting morning by morning to hear what the Father had to say to Him, to teach Him, to tell Him for His ministry.

It again brings a tremendous emphasis upon the place of the ear. We have seen something of how important the ear is in the life of the child of God, and here it comes back again in this very beautiful passage. If we are going to bring some hope into a hopeless situation, to sustain with words him that is weary, him that is ready to faint, we have to be in very close touch with the Lord: we must get everything from Him, we must have an ear opened. This does not mean simply a readiness to hear what He says, but in this case, as contrary to Israel, it means an eager readiness to do what is heard. And so, with an ear opened and responsive, a ministry of value to others arises. Before you are through the chapter, you come to those wonderful words which exhort those who walk in darkness and have no light to stay themselves upon their God, and if you put that as a part of the prophecy and make it apply to the Lord Jesus, as undoubtedly it does, it is a very wonderful thing - walking in darkness and having no light, and yet day by day in touch with the Lord so that you can help others. Well, that is simply what it amounts to. Others are going to be helped, sustained, given hope, by those who live daily in touch with the Lord, and I think that it does suggest something as to the place of the early morning quiet time, the ear opened morning by morning. I think sometimes we use that quiet time almost exclusively for talking to the Lord. I wonder if there is not also part of it to be used in listening to the Lord. *"...morning by morning, he wakeneth my ear"*, the result, others helped, a ministry of re-assurance and hope.

Part IV

Spiritual Maturity

Chapter 16

The Foundation that is Laid

Reading: Rom. 8:19,29: 1 Cor. 3:1-3; 2 Cor. 3:18; Gal. 3:26-27; 4:6,19; Eph. 1:5, 18-19; 3:18-19; 4:13; Phil. 3:12-14; Col. 1:28; Heb. 5:12-14; 6:1.

This selection of passages is quite sufficient to show that the dominating objective of the Lord for His people is full growth, the full measure of Christ. Every apostolic letter has that object in view, and every one of these apostolic letters deals with some factor related to full growth. If that is true, then surely it is incumbent upon us as the Lord's people to have His goal before us, and to be found in the same spirit as was the apostle who said, "…that I may apprehend that for which also I was apprehended of Christ Jesus". The force of that statement may not have come to our hearts. The apostle has there said in very clear and precise language that when the Lord Jesus laid hold of him, it was for something more than that he should just become a saved man. It was in relation to a goal with which there was bound up a prize, and unto that there was to be an attaining. He said that everything for him was regarded as of value only in so far as it would help him to reach that goal, and nothing was of value at all which in no way contributed to that end. So should the Lord's people be, at all times, on full stretch for the purpose for which they have been apprehended. Everywhere in the Word of God His thought for His people is set forth as being that they should come to a full measure, to full growth, to the measure of Christ.

A Fact of Great Significance

It seems to me that the New Testament assumes that increase, along the line of expansion, that is, the adding to the church, comes by spiritual increase in the church along the line of spiritual growth amongst the Lord's people. I say, it seems to be assumed, for it is a very impressive thing that the New Testament is so very largely occupied with this one thing. The fact that all these letters — every one of them — were addressed to believers with one object, that of their spiritual growth, and so many of them embody the actual word "full growth" (often in the Authorised Version translated "perfection" or "perfect"), does not mean that the church ceased to be an evangelising instrument. They were going on with their work in relation to the unsaved, but the fact is that very little is actually said about that, and what we have here as the record is all to do with the church's own spiritual increase. That is tremendously significant, and its significance is of great importance to the Lord's people. It would almost seem that the church has forgotten this. In a very considerable circle there is a great concern for the evangelism side of the church's life and work — a concern which is right and proper, and should never be less than it is, perhaps always more — but so often and so largely the essential background of that work is overlooked, namely, an indispensable building-up and teaching ministry. The result is that the church is seeking to move out to meet the world situation with inadequate spiritual resources, and is very largely weak in face of the difficulties, and the results are of such a character as hardly to be an expression of the real power of God and fullness of Christ. That by the way, however.

It is that you and I might come to recognize this, that the Lord has set before us in His Word an overwhelming amount of evidence and proof that His dominating objective for His own is full growth, and that every child of God should have that always before him. We should be concerned about spiritual maturity, and should give it the place in our hearts, in our consideration, in our concern which it evidently occupies in the heart of the Lord Himself. We have referred to fragments in the letters of Paul, which bear directly upon this matter of spiritual full growth, showing that it is the Lord's will for His people. We have said that each of these apostolic letters deals with some factor which is immediately related to that divine object, full growth. We are not going to attempt to go through all the letters at this time, but we are going to make a beginning as the Lord enables. We are coming to feel something of what Paul felt when he wrote those words, "...admonishing every man and warning every man, that we may present every man perfect (full grown, complete) in Christ".

Christ Our Righteousness

Let us look for a moment at the letter to the Romans in this very connection. We remind ourselves of the words which are in chapter 8 verses 19 and 29. This letter to the Romans lays the foundation for all the Lord's work in His own people and in relation to this end which He has in view, and which is governing all that He has to say to them, and to do with them. This letter provides the ground upon which the Lord can go forward with His work in perfecting the saints. We ask, What is that ground? We know what the theme of the letter to the Romans is, the object for which the apostle wrote it. We know that its great outstanding truth is that of righteousness by faith, or, as it is sometimes called, justification by faith. What, then, is the issue of such faith? In this letter faith is set forth as that through which we are brought to the ground of what Christ is in resurrection. He "rose again for our justification". Christ in resurrection provides the ground of our justification and our righteousness. In death He has dealt with all unrighteousness, and therefore with all that alienated and separated from God and meant condemnation, judgment and death. Having dealt with that in death, in resurrection the ground is clear of all that. Sin has been met and dealt with and all its consequences, right to the end, and in resurrection God's way is open, and there is righteousness where there was unrighteousness, communion where there was alienation, fellowship where there was distance. Christ in resurrection is the ground of our righteousness, and faith in the Lord Jesus is here shown to be that by which we are brought on to the ground of what Christ is in resurrection, and so the relationship with God is established in Christ risen, and is established unshakeably. That is the glorious issue of this chapter, as you observe.

We want to get the full force of the words at the end of chapter 8. Verses 35 to 39 must be taken in conjunction with verses 31 to 34. Now you see this unshakeable ground, this inseparable union, this indestructible life is because of what the Lord Jesus has done in His death and resurrection, and of what He is in His Person at God's right hand. I think there may have been times when we have been rather hesitant in quoting these words at the end of Romans 8. We have had a little tremor within as we have essayed to say those words and follow up: "...neither death nor life..." wondering whether we were being a little over-bold, a little overconfident; whether at some time we might not be put to the test and find that, after all, our use of the words was not unlike Peter's self-confident assertion — "I will follow thee even unto death" — we have had a catch in the declaration. I confess that has been true of me, but now I am glad to say that there is no need for hesitation. There is a ground that is settled and fixed, unshakeable in the death and resurrection of the Lord Jesus. That ground is the expression of the love of God in Christ Jesus for me; not my love for Him, not anything that I have done or can do, not anything that is in me or that I can produce, but it is all what He is, what He has done, what He has given, and what He has established in His own Person at the right hand of God. That is divine love, and that has been made to rest upon you and upon me "whom he foreknew...". He has done it all in relation to us, the thing is finished, and there is not a power in God's universe that can alter it, that can change it, that can shake it. It is something which God has done. It is a manifestation of His own love in Christ, which nothing in the creation can touch, and it is bound up with God's elect. Therefore: "Who shall lay anything to the charge of God's elect?" This chapter reaches the point where we have put faith in God on that ground. That faith brings us onto the ground of what Christ is as risen, and that means that there is not a being that can lay anything to our charge. What a position! You can find many faults in me. I may find some faults in you. We may see much that is yet of the imperfections that are ours, but you cannot bring me under condemnation and separate me from the ground of my justification. You can find all the faults that there are to be found, and can go on doing that for the rest of your life, but you cannot upset the ground of my justification before God, you cannot touch that position of my experience with Him. The blood of Jesus Christ has settled and ratified that forever. If you can tear Jesus Christ from His place at God's right hand, then you can destroy my ground of salvation, of justification, but you cannot do that. It is fixed in heaven in Him.

To be Firmly Rooted in the Foundation Essential to Full Growth

The Lord lays that as our foundation. It is a security which is ours through faith by the grace of God. That is the message of the letter to the Romans. The grace of God to us in Jesus Christ provides such a ground that no part of the creation can lay anything to our charge, can bring us under condemnation. There is no power in this universe that can disturb what God has done for us in Christ. The Word tells us to take our place in faith upon that. Do not say, Oh the trials, the difficulties, the adversities, the sufferings; life, death, principalities, and all these things! They do make such a difference to us. They come upon us. They affect us, and upset us, and we come to feel that we do not love the Lord as much as we did the other day, that we are not so much in fellowship with the Lord as we were once, and we feel that is the upsetting of things. It is nothing of the kind.

You and I must come finally to the place where we recognize that God is unchangeable, without variation, and that in the work of His cross our salvation will not move one hair's breadth; it is as surely established as His throne. On that ground our salvation rests, and faith must take hold of that. Then we are able to say, "If God be for us..." and He is for us like that. Oh, the wonder of that word, "...God... for us"! He delivered up His Son for us, and with Him gave us all things. Through His cross He has justified us from all our sins, our iniquities, and in His Son there sees us as without sin, perfected! He says, Now, if only you will let your faith come and rest upon that, and will not move away from your faith onto your own ground of what you are in yourself, but will stay there, Satan's power is destroyed over your life, and there is nothing whatever in this universe that can prevent your reaching My end. Nothing that arises, be it life, or death, or things present, or things to come, or height, or depth, or principality, or any other creation — nothing in this universe can prevent you reaching My end if you will keep your feet there in faith. That is the foundation for God, and He can never get us anywhere until we have come to that position. You know how true that is, that if there is any question, any uncertainty, any variation in any one of us at any time, we stop dead, and God is arrested, the Spirit of the Lord can go no further. While we believe God He goes on, no matter what He has to deal with. It amounts to this: Are we going to believe God or not? If we are not, then we may as well abandon everything, for everything depends upon that, upon whether we are going to believe God.

Now here is the foundation for faith. Full growth rests upon that foundation. You never make one bit of progress toward God's end until that foundation is settled. It is important that we stand upon the firm foundation of God. Do let us seek to get to this position. It is a word for believers, and more than ever perhaps a word for today, that we should come to the place where we recognize how altogether apart from variation God is. Of course, there are some people who do not vary a great deal, but there are others who know all the variations of this natural life; the variations of feelings, the variations of thoughts, the variations which come about by the circumstances around them. We find ourselves very largely influenced by how we are physically, or how circumstances are, or for some other reason; in different moods, in different states, as we think spiritually. We vary, sometimes from day to day if not from hour to hour. God is not like that. God's work is not like that. What God has accomplished in His Son by the cross and resurrection is not subject to influences of change; it stands, it is fixed. God has taken that attitude. He is not variable. If only we would come back and recognize that God is a God of infinite grace, that grace has been demonstrated to the uttermost, and it is unchanging! If we go from it, that makes no difference to it. It is the same. We come back and find God there just where we left Him. He has not moved a little bit.

This is not said to justify weakness, but to bring to a certain settled position as to the grace of God. Everything is by His grace, because of His grace, the love of God which is in Christ Jesus our Lord. If we get settled there, God can go on with His work. Full growth? Yes, when you believe God fundamentally, when you trust God, and when your trust in God is on the ground of that perfect justification which He has granted, the removal of every obstacle in the way of His full purpose. The letter to the Romans tells of that. The foundation is laid in faith for all God's purpose, and after that you move on to the superstructure. The other letters have to do with factors in full growth when the foundation is laid.

Chapter 17

Spirituality

Reading: 1 Corinthians 2

We now pass to the first letter to the Corinthians, and you will notice that the point in the letter marked by chapter 3 begins with the definite statement that the trouble at Corinth, the inclusive trouble, was spiritual immaturity. They were babes, when it was time they had passed out of babyhood. That was the trouble at Corinth.

The Spiritual Man Constituted of God

So the whole letter deals with the causes of too long delayed maturity, and with that which is the basic factor for such people with regard to spiritual growth. We can at once state what this factor is. It is the key to this whole letter, and is "spirituality". Being the key to this letter, it is, therefore, in all these circumstances, the key to full growth. Spirituality is, of course, set over against carnality. Spirituality is essential to full growth. The second chapter is full both of the fact and of the necessity. If we ask what spirituality is, that chapter will answer the question by telling us that it is a life wholly governed, taught, illumined and led by the Holy Spirit; but not as from without. This is just where we need to recognize a difference. Here it is not a matter of the Holy Spirit as an objective person or power coming along and, so to speak, putting His hand upon us and telling us things and turning us about, and giving us direction of that kind. What the apostle clearly shows in this part of his letter is that it is the kind of person we are. He speaks in this chapter of two kinds of beings, the one whom he calls the natural, or the soulical man, the other the spiritual man; one, the man who is governed by his own soul in every way, the other who is governed by the Holy Spirit through his spirit, and thereby becomes a spiritual man as over against the soulical man. So that the spiritual man here is a kind of person, and that kind of person has particular and peculiar kinds of capacities, powers, abilities. He has faculties which are not possessed by the other kind of man, the soulical man, the natural man, and he is, therefore, endowed with capacities which take you far beyond the highest range of the natural man in apprehension, in knowledge, in understanding, as well as in accomplishment.

That point must be made perfectly clear, because some people have a kind of mentality that to be wholly Spirit-governed means that the Holy Spirit in some way does all the turning about and governing, and directing, almost objectively, as from the outside. The spiritual man is not here represented as being in that position at all, but rather as having been constituted a kind of being in whom the Holy Spirit is. He is constituted a spiritual man of spiritual intelligence, who is able, by spiritual faculties and endowments, to come into a wonderful knowledge of, and fellowship with, God Himself. That is spirituality, and that is the very heart of full growth.

It is wonderful how the chronological order of these letters is entirely upset in favor of a spiritual order. In Romans you have the foundation of righteousness by faith; then comes 1 Corinthians, and it is as though you got right to the heart of the Person concerned, and having set Him in a position, you begin to constitute something in Him, to build up in Him. So that you find that it is a matter now of having been placed in Christ by faith; Christ is in you, and that is the beginning of everything, if Christ is to be fully formed. And that is the meaning of spirituality.

It is seen in this letter, on the contrary, that carnality is a mark of immaturity, and, more than that, it is a positive hindrance to spiritual progress. With that you move through the letter and you see the many marks of carnality which are marks of immaturity. We might note some of them, and this will help us to come to an understanding of what spirituality really is.

Six Marks of Carnality as Seen in 1 Corinthians

1) Leaning to natural wisdom

Here in chapters 1 and 2 especially you see that carnality is a leaning towards, and being governed by, what is natural, what is of account according to man's own natural estimate. These Corinthians evidently had a great admiration for human wisdom. They were in a center of human wisdom, and their national life was marked with much of this admiration for the wisdom of men. They were much occupied naturally in philosophical pursuits and speculations, and so it was a part of their very nature. It was Corinthian to be always leaning toward the superiority of human wisdom, and the Corinthian believers were evidently indulging in that kind of thing. We are still very greatly influenced by the strength, the power of human wisdom — and, of course, that carries power with it! With the Corinthians knowledge was power. That was their philosophy of life. The more human knowledge you have, the more you come into a place of ascendency in this world. It is a thing which puts you in a position of advantage. Human knowledge is a real vantage ground for success in this world.

The apostle strikes some very hard blows at that natural and, at the same time, carnal thing. It is natural, but when it comes into the life of a believer it is a carnal thing. The carnal is something more positive than the natural. We are what we are by nature, but when you begin to take up what we are by nature in the realm of what we are by grace, and make something of nature in the realm of grace, then you have become carnal: and that is evil. So these two chapters are very largely occupied with a tremendous unveiling of the utter foolishness of the very thing in which these believers were glorying, and the utter weakness of it all. Knowledge? Power? Getting an advantage in this world? Very well! The world in its wisdom, and in the wisdom which it called its power, crucified the Lord of glory. What do you think of that? They did it blindly. That is ignorance!

We are not going to pursue that line further. We indicate it, because it shows us a state of mind. It was the apprizing of values according to natural and worldly standards, and they were influenced by that, and that for them was carnality, and therefore immaturity. That very thing was the hindrance to their spiritual growth. Now, apart from the thing itself, the principle is this, that a leaning toward that which is natural, and, in so leaning toward it, making it a factor in our lives as the children of God, is a mark of spiritual infancy, babyhood, immaturity; but moreover, it is a positive hindrance to anything else. You may say it is hardly necessary to stress that amongst the people of God today, but I am not so sure. You know, as well as I do, that this is one of the failings of the human heart in principle. We may be perfectly convinced that the Corinthians were all wrong and that Paul was perfectly right, that it was utter foolishness in this wise world to crucify the Lord Jesus, an altogether false idea of wisdom, of knowledge, and of strength: well, we may be quite convinced of that, and it may be that we might not fall quite in that way, but in principle this thing is found in all of us.

There is a tremendous amount of trying to win a way for the Gospel, for Christ, for the Christian life by being even with the world in some way. A young man, for example, thinks that if he has something of a sportsman's training, and his achievements in the sporting world are known, that he can use that as an advantage to win men for Christ. So he does it, and he plays that off to try and win the respect, the esteem, the hearing, the ear of men, and in a way he is all the time going onto their ground and thinking that he is going to win converts in that way. It is this same thing in principle. If men can only be won along such lines they are not worth winning; you will not get the right thing. The only ground upon which a man may be really saved is upon the ground of such a need in his own heart, and recognized by him, that he will come to Christ as a matter of life and death. If he has to be won by your putting up something which appeals to him on his own ground, there will be a permanent weakness in his Christian life. Let us be careful that even in our eagerness we do not compromise a little, do not step over onto natural ground, which for us would be sheer carnality. That is Corinthian ground; it does not get beyond babyhood, the standards of men, the world's values of things; wisdom, and power, and such like.

That was the first thing in this whole matter of spirituality. Spirituality has nothing to do with that. What does Paul really mean? What does he say, in effect? He says: After all, you may go down to men, with all your worldly wisdom, and try to win them for Christ, but the natural man cannot understand the things of the Spirit of God; he is laboring under an absolute ban. Before a man can understand the things of the Spirit of God he has to be born again, and be a spiritual man in the very beginnings of his new life. He must have something that no man outside of Christ has. You are in a hopeless position if you try to get down there onto his ground: "...we received, not the spirit of the world, but the spirit which is from God; that we might know the things that were freely given to us of God" (1 Cor. 2:12). These Corinthians had the spirit of the world, and were trying to be Christians with the spirit of the world; therefore they were limited in their knowledge, their understanding, their apprehension, and remained like little babes who had never yet come to any kind of personal knowledge. All that they had was what they had been told.

2) Selectiveness on natural grounds

The next phase of this carnality is seen in chapter 3 and chapter 4. There you have selectiveness on natural grounds. It is another phase or form of the leaning toward what is natural. One says, I am of Paul; and another says, I am of Apollos; and another says, I am of

Peter; and another says, I am of Christ. The apostle deals drastically with it in these two chapters. Carnality is set forth as that kind of thing where you lean toward your own natural likes and dislikes amongst men, amongst teachings. I like Paul as a man! I like Apollos as a man! I like Paul's line of teaching! I like Apollos's wonderful eloquence! I like Peter's line! They were, according to their natural likes, selective on natural grounds, dividing up the Lord's servants and the Lord's Body. Who will be bold enough to say that he himself has never fallen into that failure? It is quite natural to have such likes and dislikes. It very often means that we have to put something to death in us to listen to some people, to have anything to do with them. We have to take ourselves in hand, and say: I must seek if there is not something there that is of the Lord, and for the time being shut my eyes to the other that offends. It is quite natural to say: I like so-and-so, and I would go anywhere to hear so-and-so, but as for the other man I cannot get on with him at all. That is carnality. "For whereas there is among you jealousy and strife, are ye not carnal, and walk after the manner of men? For when one saith, I..." — Oh, we need not go further! That is the heart of the matter, "I". It ought to be "Not I, but Christ". Is there anything of Christ here in these men? That is what we should be after. The vessel may trouble me, may sometimes give me bad times, but my natural inclinations are not the point in question at all in such a matter; that is carnality for me. I am not speaking for people who do not profess to be the Lord's, but for me it is carnality, a bringing of the natural into the realm of the spiritual, and making it a governing thing. Spirituality means that I am after whatever is of Christ, no matter in what vessel it is brought to me. Again and again it is clearly to be seen in the Word of God that, had men taken account of the means by which God came to them, they would have lost the blessing, and some were dangerously near that, and some did lose it.

Israel lost the blessing for that very reason. They were offended with the Man Christ Jesus. "Is not this the carpenter?..." Had He been some glorious potentate from heaven they would have received the message! Let us be careful. God tests us very often as to the reality of our hearts, as to whether they are set upon Himself, by bringing us a great blessing wrapped up in a very unacceptable wrapping.

Spirituality is the opposite of leaning toward natural selectiveness, likes and dislikes. If you and I desire to go on to full growth, this is one of the things that has to be recognized and dealt with. It is a case of just setting aside our natural life in the interests of the spiritual. Such an opportunity is with us every day. Spirituality is determined by how far we are ready to be led.

3) Lack of moral sensibility

We pass on to chapter 5. It is a terrible chapter. Carnality is here shown to us in a defectiveness of moral sensibility. We are not going to stay with it, and yet we should not just ignore it. Spirituality must work out in real moral sensibility, sensitiveness, in such a way that there is a mighty reaction in us from those tendencies of nature that are downward in the moral sense. We are not talking about not being tempted. Everyone is tempted (though it is not good). The very fact that we carry with us a nature which is not wholly purged from the roots and fibers of sin and the fall, constitutes a ground upon which temptation comes to us. There is no sin in temptation. At times there may be some weakening; we may be more open for various reasons to weakness than at other times, but the point is this, that spirituality represents in us a revolt and a reaction that in the presence of moral weakness turns round, reacts against that. That is the work of the Spirit of God in us, making us spiritual. At Corinth there was not only the one who defaulted (we are not going to judge that one), but what the apostle was troubled about was that the assembly had not sufficient moral sensitiveness to deal with that thing, and he had to write them a strong letter to pull them up sharply upon moral grounds, to cleanse the assembly. They did not do it until Paul practically made them do it. There was a low and inadequate moral sensitiveness about the assembly; there was not a sufficient measure of spirituality to react violently to that thing, and say: We are defiled, we must put this away; we must purge ourselves; we must stand before God without judgment in this matter. They did not do it; they tolerated it, they let it go.

We are not applying this in any assembly way just now, but are just saying that spirituality means a strong reaction to the encouragement of anything unclean. I do not know how necessary it might be to say a thing like that. There are various forms of low moral sense, but in a spiritual person, and in a spiritual assembly there will be something which reacts against that, in conversation, in talk, in looseness of any kind. Spirituality lifts onto a much higher level. That again, then, is carnality, and no individual life and no assembly of the Lord's people can grow to the fullness of Christ without that spiritual sensitiveness which feels bad in the presence of anything morally loose.

4) A spirit of variance

We are not going to take up this next point at length, but we notice that Paul in chapter 6 comes to that kind of carnality which shows itself in wronging one another, and then trying to obtain one's rights by lawsuits. He commences by speaking of the lawsuits in verse 1, but he gets behind that as he goes on and says that they are robbing one another. Any kind of suit before the world, or in the church, ought to be rendered unnecessary by the getting rid of this wronging of one another. What a low level amongst the Lord's people is revealed when they rob one another.

There are more ways than one of robbing the Lord's people, but it is the principle that is in view, the failing to recognize the rights of the Lord's children. If it is wrong for a child of God to stand up for his rights, and to fight for them, it is equally wrong that the rights of the Lord's people should be ignored or set at naught. There is an honoring of one another, and that of which Paul speaks elsewhere, a looking of everyone, not upon his own things, but upon the things of others; that is, taking into account that others also have a right to be honored, to be respected, to be given a place. It seems that the spirit here at Corinth was that of the individual seeking to have the advantage, even at the expense of another believer. It is the spirit of the thing that is the trouble behind it all. Spirituality would be just the opposite of this, that even if one were wronged one would not fight for one's rights, especially before the world. Spirituality would mean, in an assembly and amongst the Lord's people, and on the part of each individual, a mutual recognition and holding in honor because — as Paul leads this whole thing out, as we shall see in a moment — we are members one of another, members of the Body.

I like the wisdom of the Holy Spirit through His servant Paul, as this whole matter is headed up to chapter 12. Just imagine one member of the Body going to law against another member of the same Body! What sense would there be in one hand fighting the other hand, or in my fist assailing any other part of my body? That is perhaps a crude way of putting it, but Paul now applies the point in that way and says: You are all members of one Body, and you are all interdependent, you cannot do without one another, and that member that will go to law with another is but robbing himself. It is so foolish, so senseless, so weak! All such things are evidence of a poor level of spiritual life. Spirituality will show itself in recognizing the value of every member, and, rather than in doing a member harm, in respecting and honoring that member, because of the necessity for that one. We need one another, and therefore it is the utmost childishness in a spiritual sense to be at variance with one another. Spiritual maturity will never condone that course. If we did but know it, our attitude towards another child of God comes back upon ourselves, and becomes our attitude towards ourselves. That is how God orders it, because the Holy Spirit is the Spirit who governs and balances the whole Body.

I think there is no realm in which the laws of God operate more immediately and directly than in the Body of Christ. "He that soweth unto his... flesh shall of the flesh reap corruption; but he that soweth unto the Spirit, shall of the Spirit reap everlasting life".

"Whatsoever a man soweth, that shall he also reap". Within the church of God those laws operate in a very immediate and direct way. Spirituality takes all that into account and says: I am not going to injure my own spiritual growth by doing harm to another member of Christ; I am not going to be robbed of God's end for me by failure to recognize that another also should be helped towards that end.

5) Failure to discern the Body

In chapters 10 and 11 we come to the failure to discriminate (discern) the Lord's Body. It is all wrapped up in the long discussion of things offered to idols, and that point where one thing ends and another thing begins. The Lord's Table in the apostolic days was not like our Table of the Lord. We gather to the Lord's Table and there is something quite distinct, quite by itself; there is no mistaking what that represents. In apostolic times they took their meal together, and at a certain point in their meal time they stopped and worshipped, and for the purpose took of the same food as they had been eating and drinking; they turned their ordinary meal into a corporate worshipping of the Lord. The apostle here says, You may come in hungry to your meal, and sit down and eat heartily, and just overstep the line, and in so doing confuse the two things and make that which represents the Lord's Body and the Lord's Blood a part of your feasting to the gratification of your own appetite. We are not in the same position to fall quite into the same snare, but there is a principle bound up with it upon which the Lord through His apostle puts His finger.

Terrible things resulted from that in the Corinthian church: for this cause many were sick, and not a few died. There was this other element, as we have noted, that a good deal of what they were eating and drinking in the ordinary way had already been offered in the shambles, and had already been offered to heathen gods, and they were not discriminating. But the principle underlying is this, that this loaf, this cup, speak of two things. Firstly, they speak of the covenant relationship with the Lord, in which everything in our lives is for the Lord, and in which the Lord is everything to us; we have gone out, and Christ has come in, and for us Christ is the center and the sphere, the sole object of our lives. They also speak of this, that Christ's Body, the church, has taken its place in our interest as that upon which the love of Christ is set, even unto death. "Christ loved the church, and gave himself up for it." It is "the church of God, which he purchased with his own blood". Again, it is written, "Husbands, love your wives, even as Christ also loved the church, and gave himself up for it; that he might sanctify it, having cleansed it by the washing of water with the word, that he might present the church to himself a glorious church, not having spot or wrinkle or any such thing..." The attitude of the believers toward the church is to be the attitude of Christ toward the church. Spirituality is that which, on the one hand, gives Christ His place over all that is personal, and enables us to subordinate everything to His interests. There was a failure in this respect at Corinth, and a yielding to personal gratification, instead of glorying in the Lord. Spirituality is just the opposite of that, and so spirituality is a mark of growth. We shall never come to full growth spiritually if we are just going to be governed by our natural appetites.

Then, on the other hand, spirituality is marked by love of all the Lord's people. At Corinth, again, there was failure to recognize Christ's love for His church. Their attitude one toward another was therefore anything but that of Christ for His own, and so they did not discern the one Body as represented at the Table. Paul says, "The loaf which we break, is it not our common participation in the body of Christ? Seeing that we, who are many, are one loaf, one body: for we all partake of the one loaf." The Lord's Table is the Body in representation. We must recognize that Christ's object of love and devotion is His Church, and have the same love and devotion to His people and for His people as He had. Let us put that quite simply. A truly large spiritual life is marked by a great devotion to the Lord's people, to the Body of Christ, as over against an undue measure of individualism.

6) The coveting of spiritual gifts for personal ends

The last feature of carnality which we will note is that which comes up in chapter 7 in connection with spiritual gifts. It is strange that this matter should come up into the realm of carnality and spiritual immaturity, and yet it does. I do not see how we can get away from the fact, if we honestly read this chapter, that the apostle was dealing with this very matter of spiritual gifts from the same standpoint as he was dealing with the other things at Corinth. What was the trouble? It is one which perhaps we think we need not fear. The first part of chapter 12 indicates where the trouble was. We cannot stay with verses 1-3, to consider them in detail, but there is a great deal there that it would be very much to our good to recognize. On the face of it there is this: these Corinthians before they came to the Lord were pagans to this degree that they were occupied with spiritism, and in spiritism (often termed "spiritualism") there is a definite system of counterfeit Holy Ghost activity. Spiritism as we know it today can produce speaking in tongues, and all the other things, such as powers, miracles, and so on. The whole system here is counterfeited in spiritism. I believe that spiritism is going to be the great ally of Antichrist, the counterfeit of Christ, and the Holy Spirit, and thereby many will be carried away. The paganism of these Corinthians is seen in their being carried away to those dumb idols, and in connection with idol worship there were spirit manifestations, and they came under a false Holy Spirit (if we may use that term). The Greek is striking there, and it is perfectly in keeping with the thought of coming under a spiritual power, so that you act and speak as under control. The apostle is here using it concerning people who are under the control of a power. If you are under the control of an evil spirit you will not say, "Jesus is Lord". The evil spirit will not say that.

The point is this, that there was not amongst these people at Corinth a clear discrimination between spiritism and the Holy Spirit. Here you have come to the heart of the trouble. They had been in the false thing, and had now come into the true thing, and were not discriminating. Why were they not discriminating? Because they were so taken up with experiences, manifestations, demonstrations, sensations, that which is apparent evidence of something. That is the danger. The danger is of wanting an experience, wanting a proof, wanting to have a sensation. That is carnality, and you will mix the Holy Spirit up with spiritism if you are not careful along that line, and multitudes are doing it. The devil is getting his advantage along that line in many people. They think it is the Holy Spirit when it is a false thing, simply because they want something. That is why the apostle goes so steadily at this matter. He says in effect: "Be careful; do not put things in their wrong place; do not give importance to things which are not so important as you think they are. Speaking in tongues is not so important as you are making it out to be. It is one of the least of the gifts."

Do you see the point? You have to recognize the meaning of these first three verses in chapter 12. It was failure to discriminate between the true Holy Ghost and the false.

Then as to the rest of the chapter, we see from verse 12 to verse 27 that they were not recognizing the relatedness of gifts. That is the safeguard, to recognize that. There are the gifts of the Holy Spirit, real, genuine, and true; we are not going to put them aside because of false gifts. At the same time we have to watch the balance, we have to have spiritual understanding, spiritual wisdom in this matter. The Corinthians were taking the things as personal, in a detached and individual way, and making something of them because it was a wonderful and marvelous experience: and with them it all ended there. Why did Paul write the whole of that section on the Body of Christ, and why did he come into it so livingly? "There are diversities of gifts, *BUT* (now comes the check — everyone is glorying in that phase of the diversity that has come to them) the same Spirit…" "There are diversities of ministrations, but the same Lord". "There are diversities of workings, but the same God who worketh all things in all". You need to weigh every fragment — it is "the same God who worketh all things" in all the members, in all the Body — "To each one is given the manifestation of the Spirit to *PROFIT WITHAL*". Then when you have enumerated the gifts you come to this statement: "For as the body is one… so also is the Christ." The article is used there. You have got to the heart of things. Spiritual gifts? Yes! What for? For me to glory in, to be gratified by, to talk about *MY* experience? Ah, this is the test. Is the whole Body profiting? Is the one Lord being glorified? Is this whole matter related and working out to mutual increase? This is a corporate matter, not an individual matter at all. If you detach it and take it out of its relatedness, you divide its end, which end is the building up of the whole Body and the mutual increase. What is the result at Corinth? They have made this whole thing an individual, personal matter, unrelated, in which they themselves glory. They came perilously near to a most awful sin in failing to discriminate between spiritism and the Holy Ghost, all by reason of their desire, their love for something that brought a sense of satisfaction to themselves, pleasure to themselves, gratification to themselves. That is carnality. That is immaturity.

All that may be in a measure instructive or enlightening, but you see how strongly this letter comes down upon the need for real spirituality, and what spirituality is. Spirituality does not hold anything of the Lord's for itself, and never makes anything from the Lord the ground of its own pleasure and gratification, and personal, individual, unrelated glorying. Spirituality holds everything in relation to all saints, unto the increase of Christ. It sees no value in anything apart from that. So the apostle goes on with his corrective.

Two things stand out when you have taken the whole of this letter.

The Natural Man Wholly Put Away in the Cross

First of all right at the beginning the cross sets aside the natural man absolutely. "I determined to know nothing among you save Jesus Christ, and him crucified". Paul acted upon the principle of the cross when he said, "I was with you in weakness and much... trembling..." There was nothing in Paul naturally, had he desired to come on to that ground, that would have enabled him to be amongst them in anything other than of weakness and fear and much trembling. But he was acting on the principle of the cross. He says it was deliberately done in order that their faith might not stand in the wisdom of men, but in the power of God. What they needed to know was the difference between natural power, wisdom, and all that is of nature, and the true power of God in the Holy Ghost. The cross sets aside the whole life of nature, and opens the way for spirituality and full growth.

The Essence of Spirituality is Love

Secondly, when all has been said, the essence of spirituality is love (chapter 13). "Though I speak with the tongues of men (terrestrial voices) and of angels (tongues not known amongst men, heavenly language), and have not love" — I am a most spiritual person? Not at all! — I have made a great deal of progress in spiritual life? Not at all! I am what? "I am become sounding brass, or a clanging cymbal." So much, then, for an entire want of spirituality, even though you may have tongues. Paul writes the word "nothing" over a great many things that we naturally would think were very important: faith to remove mountains, the giving of the body to be burned, and so on — he writes "nothing" over every one of them. Not that they are of no account in themselves; these things are of account in their place, and in their connection, but if they are without love they are "nothing". The essence of spirituality is not the gifts, it is the grace. We are not going to choose between gifts and graces, between gifts and love. That is not the point of all. The apostle does not intend us to take this attitude: Oh well, give me love; I do not want gifts. I let go of all the gifts if you will only give me the love. Paul is trying to make it clear that these things in themselves can be held carnally. Really to reach the end for which God gives them they must be held spiritually, and the essence of spirituality is love. It covers everything.

We go back to the beginning now, and start again: Wisdom, strength, divisions, schisms, lusts, all of them go out when love comes in. So he closes thus: "The grace of the Lord Jesus and the love of God, and the fellowship of the Holy Spirit be with you all." That is what you Corinthians need. Undoubtedly the apostle summed it all up in what we call the "Benediction".

Chapter 18

The Way to Divine Knowledge

Reading: 2 Cor. 3; Rom. 8:19,29; 5:17-19; 3:12; 4:6; Gen. 2:17; 3:4-7.

In those passages you have the parts of a wonderful revelation. First of all, there is God's thought and intention: His Son, His image, His fullness; the standard, the model, the completeness. Then you have believers conformed to the image of His Son, and the whole creation brought into being in relation to that purpose, it's very meaning and object found in the intention of God as to His Son, and man's conformity to His image. So that the whole creation is, as it were, made to hang upon one central purpose, man in the image of God's Son.

Life and Light

Two things become the great governing factors and principles by which the purpose was to be realized; the one life, the other light. "God who commanded the light to shine out of darkness," planted a tree of life, open to man, and a tree of light (the tree of the knowledge of good and evil) which, while man was under probation, was kept from him, under a prohibition. It is well to remember that true light only comes along the line of the obedience of faith. It was not that God was withholding essential knowledge from man, but was testing him as to his faith in Himself, and as to his obedience of faith.

We have seen how things proceeded. Man ceased at a certain point to believe and obey God, and believed and obeyed God's adversary instead, and man's disbelief and the disobedience were in the direction of having knowledge and light for his own ends and glory, that he should have the seat of glory and power and wisdom in himself, and become something. When you have recognized that you have got to the heart of everything, for God never intended man to have that in himself, but only in His Son. The glory and the wisdom, the knowledge and the power are all bound up with His Son, Jesus Christ, and never to be had apart. Man essayed to possess it all himself, to have it in himself, so that he would become independent in God's universe. So he struck for light and knowledge, for self-glory and empowerment, and exaltation. The result was immediate death. "In the day that thou eatest thereof thou shalt surely die". There was no postponing of things. Death took place that day, and the evidence of the death from that day onward is blinding, darkness or ignorance; just the opposite of what they aimed at, and struck for. Even when we come to Israel in the wilderness in the presence of a great revelation of God's glory, we read that their minds were hardened, and a veil was upon their hearts; and that veil remains.

All that, of course, is the working out of a deeply laid plot, a plot to defeat God in His purpose, to cheat Him of His end, to frustrate the realization of His intention concerning His Son. The history of this world is the history of a rivalry between the Son of God and Satan; divine purpose fixed in Christ, divine purpose assailed by Satan, and the assault always directed against the Son of God, revealing that Satan's great object is to have the place which God has given to the Son. So that this is just the outworking of that plot, that evil device.

Now we come to this second letter to the Corinthians. It has a tremendous background and you will see how very great is its significance and its value. Oh, how much there is behind this letter. Here is a man sitting down to his spiritual correspondence, writing to believers a personal letter, and as he writes the Spirit of God takes him back into the past eternity and into the counsels of God, touching all the deep, mighty elements of the drama of the ages. When you read the letter for the first time, it looks like so many personal things said by one man to a few friends, but if you dwell upon it, meditate upon it, it expands, and expands, and you find yourself taken right back into the heart of God before times eternal, and on through the past ages and up to the cross of the Lord Jesus, and out from the cross on through this dispensation, and still on to the consummation of all things. It is all in one simple letter.

We come, then, to this letter, and with but a few touches there flash out these great thoughts of God. We commenced with the verse so well-known in chapter 5: "Wherefore if any man is in Christ, there is a new creation: the old things are passed away; behold, they are become new" (verse 17, R.V. margin). God is here seen beginning all over again. The creation missed its way. Its course was foiled, the purpose of God in it was interrupted, it went astray. Creation is bound to a divine purpose, but even if in the straightway of that divine purpose it has not the urge of that purpose unto consummation, while if it has gone out of the way it is like a person within whom is a groaning to get back. "The whole creation groaneth and travaileth..." What for? "...waiting for the manifestation of the sons of God." "The earnest expectation of the creation" is still bound up with God's purpose. That creation has gone astray. The purpose of God cannot be set aside, and therefore there must, if needs be, be a new creation, and that in Christ Jesus.

"God, that said, Light shall shine out of darkness..." (We are back at the creation.) For what purpose was this? That His Son, the fullness and the express image of His thought and intention for man, should give character to the race, and that we should be conformed to that image. God said light should shine out of darkness, and that was His first act in the direction of that purpose. Now you leap right into it here, without ages between: "...hath shined into our hearts, to give the light of the knowledge of the glory of God in the face of

Jesus Christ". You have all the divine thought and intent, and the divine end, reached in Jesus Christ. There is a new creation, a creation with a purpose, which is conformity to the image of God's Son. How is it to be reached? By life. Put your pencil line underneath each occurrence of the word "life" in this second letter to the Corinthians. You will be surprised how many times that word occurs, and you will notice that it is always life out of death. The apostle is speaking much of his own experience. "We despaired even of life." Ah yes, but there was an object in God's bringing him there. What was the object? "…that we should not trust in ourselves, but in God which raiseth the dead." "Always bearing about in the body the dying of Jesus, that the life also of Jesus may be manifested in our mortal flesh." Life works in you as the result of our dying! There is much more about life coming out of death with which we will not stay at this time. Then there is light out of darkness: life and light in relation to the new creation, with this end in view, conformity to the image of God's Son.

All those elements are quite clear, and you can piece them together. Our purpose is to bring it down to quite a precise application.

God's Purpose and its Realisation

Firstly, God's intention. An attaining unto the full measure of Christ as God's standard is His intention. We are told definitely that "whom he foreknew, he also foreordained" to that end, "to be conformed to the image of his Son, that he might be the firstborn among many brethren".

Secondly, the way to its realization. The apostle sums all up in one central thing in the creation, giving the creation its meaning and its value, namely, the revelation of Jesus Christ in us.

Now you see the movement. In Romans relatedness to God is secured anew through the work of Christ in His cross; righteousness, which is by faith. Those who were separated, afar off, alienated through sin and wicked works, are made nigh by His blood, and union with God in Christ is established; deliverance from all that which had come in to frustrate the divine purpose, deliverance from the dead man: "O wretched man that I am, who shall deliver me from the body of this death? I thank God through Jesus Christ our Lord." So the relationship is renewed and established through faith on the ground of righteousness.

In the first letter to the Corinthians a man indwelt by the Holy Spirit, and endowed with spiritual capacities for knowing the things of God, is seen. As the apostle says, "We have not received the spirit of the world, but the spirit which is of God, that we might know the things which are... given us by God." That is enablement, empowerment, that is faculty for spiritual knowledge, for spiritual things; the man is there. Now that is what is to go on in that man. What is the central thing that is to be the object of those faculties? For what are those faculties given? They are given for an apprehension of Jesus Christ. In a word it all amounts to this, that to reach God's end, to come to that fullness of our foreordination according to His foreknowledge, there must be that inward revelation of Jesus Christ which is constantly expanding. All growth is bound up with that, and so the apostle bases the whole of this argument upon the one point, namely, that "God... hath shined in our hearts, to give the light of the knowledge of the glory of God in the face of Jesus Christ". I take that phrase "the face of Jesus Christ" to mean that Jesus Christ is an image or portrait of God's glorious thought. It is only a figurative word, which does not mean actually his countenance. The face is the representation: it is the man. The knowledge of the glory of God is in the face of Jesus Christ, and that has to come into us by revelation. Every inch of ground in spiritual progress that you and I will cover, every bit of advance in spiritual increase will be upon the basis of some fresh revelation of Jesus Christ in our hearts — not truth to our minds but the revelation of the person in our hearts. God has bound up everything with His Son in person, and there can be no light, no knowledge and no life leading to God's end apart from the revelation of Jesus Christ. Thus spiritual progress, spiritual increase just resolves itself into a question of the unveiling of Jesus Christ in our hearts by the Holy Spirit, so that as we go on we are able to say: "I am seeing more and more of what the Lord Jesus is, and who He is in the divine thought, and that seeing for me is enlargement, is increase, is strength, is life, is power." It is all such a thing as that.

The Proof of Experience

You see the apostle takes an illustration. He takes us back to Israel at Horeb, and tells us of Moses going into the Mount, of his receiving the law and coming down with some of the light on his face, and standing before the congregation and reading the law, and of the glory being too much for them to look upon, so that he had to put a veil over his face. He read a law which itself was in glory, given in glory and accompanied by glory, albeit a glory that was departing. What was the effect? It was, as we have said, written by the finger of God, it was accompanied by glory, it was an unveiling of the divine mind for His people. Everything was very wonderful; it spoke of God, had all the accompaniments of heaven with it: but what was the effect? Death! Condemnation! That very generation perished in the wilderness, and never came to the end which God had fixed for it. God had referred to the land flowing with milk and honey, with fullness. That was His thought, His intention, His purpose. He covenanted to give them the land. Then came the revelation of His mind as to the way in which they could come into His thought and intention for them, and they perished in the wilderness and never reached the land. Why? Because there was not only a veil over the face of Moses, but there was a veil over their hearts. They had not had the eyes of their hearts enlightened. They had not received a spirit of wisdom and revelation in the knowledge of Him.

The apostle takes that right up and comes immediately to the question of the new creation, and says: "Things are different now;

there is no need that anyone should perish in the wilderness today. Here is the so much greater advantage which secures God's end." What is it? It is not something presented to you in your impotence and helplessness, but a revelation given within you, Christ who is God's full intention revealed within you. It is not something objective to which we are journeying; it is Christ within, the hope of glory. It is not something into which we have to strive day by day, but an inward reality. Christ is revealed within, and when you see Him, you are in the land. You have come right into living touch with God's end. What remains? Only that what is within you should be expanding from day to day, growing, increasing, until Christ (as the apostle puts it) is fully formed in you, and you, not now beholding Him in some objective way, but by the Holy Spirit in your own hearts seeing the Lord Jesus in a growing way, are changed into the same image from one degree of glory to another, conformed to the image of God's Son. It all hangs upon this: "God... hath shined into our hearts..." God has made this whole thing in His purpose now an inward thing by the Holy Spirit. How near we are to it. How marvelous is the possibility of reaching God's end. The apostle here says, in effect: "That is the basis of all our ministry. We are not talking from a book; we are not, like Moses reading from tables of stone; we are not just reciting something which God has written; we are now living out something that God has done within". That is ministry. "We have this ministry." That is something that is coming from the inside.

Now let us see how far we have, for real practical ends, grasped the significance of this. Let us start at the beginning. Can you really associate yourself with these words: "God... hath shined into our hearts to give the light of the knowledge of the glory of God in the face of Jesus Christ"? You can put it in other words if you like, if that seems too wonderful. Can you really say, I know the Lord Jesus in a living way within my own heart? Then you have all the fullness summed up in that, and all that you need to reach God's end is that you should discover what you have; not seek that God will give you more, but that God will show you what you have in Christ, what Christ is. There is such a fullness in Christ that it will take so much longer than the longest life that we could live here on this earth to discover anything worthwhile comparatively of what Christ is. I am quite certain that the one effect left upon us of a growing knowledge of the Lord Jesus will be that we feel we are only on the edge of things all the time. However long we live, and however long that goes on, we are only on the edge of things. I am sure that is true in the case of those who are discovering something more of the Lord Jesus. I can say that my most recent discovery of the Lord brought me to the place where I wondered if I had ever known Him before. It almost makes you feel that you have been wasting your time when you get a new revelation of the Lord Jesus. That is how it will always be. It is a wonderful thing to have a revelation of God in Christ in your own heart, and it is a wonderful thing if that revelation is opening out, growing from day to day as you go on. Do believe that, while it may sound to you a thing altogether too high for you, it is meant to be of the greatest and simplest help to you.

You young people have a high standard put before you, the whole thing seems so immense, and so difficult, that you wonder if ever you will reach it, and sometimes you perhaps feel the burden of it all, and do not feel you will ever attain. Now let us get rid of all that burden, and all that worry, and come right back to the secret of everything that God ever intended for you. It is this: "Christ in you, the hope of glory." Have you despaired of reaching that glory? Well, the hope of glory is Christ in you. There is hope. If you look upon the old creation, that old creation of which you are a part, and which is in you, you despair. Christ in you is the hope of glory. There is a new creation in Christ Jesus. If you have the basic thing you have the root of the matter. We do not mean that thing of which a great many people are talking in their modernism, about the Christ in every man. We mean that definite act of faith in Christ Jesus, and His work on the cross, by which you receive Him into your life and are thereby born again and made a new creation. If that has taken place, and you know that Christ is in you, you have the root of the matter. Everything in the outworking of divine purpose related to that is simply a matter of your seeking to know the Lord Jesus Christ in all that He is as your fullness for every day.

The Path of Discovery

As you look at this second letter to the Corinthians, you see that it begins another chapter in this very thing, and you look at the apostle Paul himself there, because he is brought into view as a practical example of this truth. You will see what is implied when we speak of learning to know what it means that Christ has been revealed within. See this apostle, in whom Christ is, in whom Christ has been revealed, taken into definite situations, trying circumstances, deep waters, through much suffering, and as he passes that way I see that all that upon which he might count and reckon in himself and in this world to get him through is breaking down. He comes to a place where he himself cannot go on any further, and he knows it; he cannot take another step, he cannot put forth another effort. If this man had ever acted upon the strength of his own will — and, you know, some people can do an immense amount by their will power, and I think Paul did something in that way sometimes — if ever he had been so actuated by his own will as a strong-willed man, making up his mind that he would do it if he died in the attempt, he got to the end, where he could not make another effort, he despaired of life. Then it was that he made a discovery, that that was not the end but the beginning. When he got to the end himself there was "God who raiseth the dead".

He discovered Christ in him as the risen One in the power of resurrection, and to have made that discovery had a wonderful result. In what way? "We have this ministry." The whole of this second letter to the Corinthians is on the ministry. What is this ministry? It is the ministry of life being ministered, the life of the risen Lord who has been discovered as life, discovered in the hour of death. The energy of His risen life was discovered in the hour when all his own energy had come to an end. Yes, the light of that risen life breaking upon him when he was in a corner and did not know which way to turn, and felt that he was shut in and there was no way out. He discovered that the Lord had a way out, the Lord had ways of which he was entirely ignorant, the Lord knew more than he did.

To make that discovery sometimes is good. Somehow or other we are always coming up against the fact that the Lord knows more than we do, and knows better than we do. That is discovering what Christ in you is. It is very practical. It is something for every day. Believe me, the Lord is taking you and me along such a path with the one object (Oh, let this be written in our hearts!) of making us discover what a Christ we have; and as we discover Him, what He is to us in every circumstance, in every need, in every hour of despair and weakness, and helplessness, that is the increase of Christ. That means that something more of the Lord has become our life, and that kind of thing goes on. That is why the Lord presses us so much, deals with us as He does. The greatest discoveries have been made in the greatest trial, and the deepest distress of heart. We have come out with a fuller measure of the Lord. That is what constitutes ministry, Paul says here. "We have this ministry", and "We have this treasure in vessels of fragile clay..." and that is necessary in order that "the exceeding greatness of the power may be of God and not of ourselves". It is all of God. It is revealed in Christ.

We have touched upon the mere fringe of this whole glorious matter. We see that "the earnest expectation of the creation waiteth for the revealing" of this that God is today doing in secret, under cover. The world is not seeing, and we ourselves do not always see what God is doing in us, but there is going to be a day of manifestation. It is the day when sonship is manifested, and sonship is not just some kind of formal relationship to God. Sonship is a nature developed, a likeness produced. The day of the manifestation of that likeness to His Son is coming, and the whole creation will heave a great sigh of relief and say, We have arrived at last!

That is God's end, the revelation of His Son in us, our conformity to His image, the hope, the assurance. "God… hath shined into our hearts, to give the light of the knowledge of the glory of God in the face of Jesus Christ."

Chapter 19

The Incentive to Maturity

Reading: Romans 8:19,29; 1 Cor. 3:1-3; 2 Cor. 3:18; Gal. 3:26; 4:6,19.

We have already pointed out how much there is of strength and urgency in the New Testament concerning full spiritual growth. Indeed, more than ninety percent of the New Testament is addressed to believers for that very purpose. Every letter of Paul's is a strong urge in that direction, and was written specifically for the increase of Christ in the believers, that they might come to full growth, to the stature of the fullness of Christ.

We observed that this is not only true in a general way, but that every letter of the apostle deals with the matter of spiritual growth from a different standpoint, or has a particular aspect of that matter to deal with, which, of course, has its occasion in the situation existing in the different places to which the letters were sent.

Then we began to consider the letters of Paul in their bearing upon this matter, and we got to the end of the second letter to the Corinthians. If the Lord wills, we will presently review that ground as we approach the letter to the Galatians, but we want to say another word first concerning the urgency of this matter.

Why Maturity is so Vital

It does not require argument and evidence to be produced to convince you that this is a matter of very great importance from the

Lord's standpoint. It is quite impossible to read the New Testament and fail to see that it is to this end the Lord is by His Word and Spirit urging believers all the time, making it perfectly manifest that the Lord's thought is not just the salvation of men from sin and from judgment. The greater emphasis with the Lord is what they are saved unto, rather than what they are saved from. It is divine purpose which is always governing, and the calling by His grace is according to His purpose: "according to the eternal purpose". We must remember that salvation, from start to finish, at every point, is related to divine purpose, is toward an end, is with something in view, and in order to reach that which is in view in divine purpose a going on with God unto full spiritual measure is necessary.

There again it needs to be said, that to have full grown people is not an end in itself. The end in view is that they may be prepared and fitted for the purpose unto which He has called. No mere spiritual infant, who is such beyond the point of time where infancy ought to have ceased, can come into the divine purpose, and that is the reason why there is this tremendous emphasis placed upon the tragedy of immaturity when it ought to be otherwise, and upon the necessity for maturity. It is with something of a groan that the apostle writes these words to the Corinthians: "And I, brethren, could not speak unto you as unto spiritual, but as unto carnal, as unto babes". Now it is all right to speak to babes when they are rightly such, but when it is time they were more than babes it is a terrible thing to have to go on speaking to them thus.

So that we must see what the purpose of God through maturity is, before we can feel the real weight and recognize the real importance of full spiritual growth. What is the purpose of God? What is that eternal purpose to which we are called by His grace in Christ Jesus? There are several words in the New Testament which are very full words, and very significant words. There is the word "adoption", a very misunderstood word by us, because it means something entirely different in our Western language from what it means in the New Testament. There is another word "sons"; and, again, another word "inheritance". If you look at those words you will find that they are always related to a particular thing. They are related to a position in the ages to come, and that position is definitely stated to be dominion over the inhabited earth. That governs everything in the thought of God. You will remember that in the second chapter of the letter to the Hebrews that is clearly and definitely stated: "...not unto angels did he subject the inhabited earth to come, whereof we speak. But one in a certain place hath testified, saying, What is man that thou art mindful of him — *puttest him in charge?*". The inhabited earth to come will be subjected to man, and it is that particular man which is God's object in this specific dispensation. It is the corporate man in Christ; the church which is His Body, conformed to the image of God's Son, of whom He is the firstborn, as the firstborn among many brethren. Thus the letter to the Hebrews goes on to say that in bringing many sons to glory the Author of their salvation was made perfect through sufferings.

Galatians and the Day of the Adoption

That brings us right to this letter to the Galatians. You will notice in the course of this letter that the apostle Paul lights upon Abraham, and takes up everything in relation to Abraham, and in so doing he throws back our horizon tremendously. To begin with, he gets rid of a whole dispensation, the Jewish dispensation, which came between Abraham and Christ. He leaps right over it, pushes it on one side, and gets back into the universal. He says, in effect, "That was a merely local thing, a merely temporal thing. It came in, it served a purpose, and it is now done with. Now let us go back to Abraham, and take things up there. That is where things began, and we come in with Abraham." "Know therefore", he concludes, "that they which be of faith, the same are sons of Abraham".

You will know that there is a great similarity between this letter and the letter to the Romans. The subject is almost identical, the object the same. The letter to the Romans is a more thorough-going treatise (if we may call it that) on the subject of law and grace. The letter to the Galatians is an impassioned outburst of righteous indignation. The spirit of the apostle is aflame at the outrages against the work of God which were being perpetrated, to which we will refer later. The object is the same, and if you go back to the fourth chapter of the Romans you have this remarkable word: "Now the promise to Abraham that he should be heir of the world..." You have no such thing recorded in the Old Testament. Nothing in the Old Testament says that God made promise to Abraham that he should be heir of the world in this sense. It is there that the apostle takes things up with Abraham. In his letter to the Galatians, he deals with everything along the line of sonship, adoption, heirs of the promise made to Abraham. That is inheritance. When you have grasped that, and recognized what that means, you are getting into the flaming heart of the apostle. We cannot get into this letter unless we understand and recognize the tremendous background of it. In a word, what we are presented with is this: God made a promise to Abraham that he should be heir of the world. Upon that we are told that Abraham looked for a city whose builder and maker was God, and we find Abraham refusing all the cities of this world, choosing to dwell in tents with Isaac and Jacob who were also the heirs of the promise; repudiating this world and its cities, because he looked for a city whose builder and maker was God, with the promise that he should be heir of the world.

Now we look at the apostle's argument in this letter to the Galatians. Who is a Jew? Not he who is one naturally. He is a Jew who is linked with Abraham's seed by faith. "Not unto seeds", says the apostle, "but... to thy seed, which is Christ." Abraham's seed is Christ. Faith in Jesus Christ constitutes us the seed of Abraham. One of the last clauses of this letter to the Galatians refers to the Israel of God, and leading up to that is all this about the "Jerusalem that is beneath, that is in bondage with her children, and the Jerusalem which is above and is free, which is the mother of us all". He looked for a city. We are Abraham's seed by faith in Jesus Christ, related to a city, and that city is to govern the world. The end of the Word of God makes it perfectly clear that the heavenly city, the new Jerusalem, is the church, and in this whole dispensation the church is the object upon which God's heart is set, in order that she may govern the inhabited earth in the ages to come. That is the purpose. That government demands full spiritual growth, and because of the greatness, the seriousness, and the importance of God's eternal purpose as to the government of this world, if in heart you enter into that with God, you also will become aflame as did the apostle, when you discover there are things which are working insidiously against God's purpose in the saints, to frustrate spiritual full growth. Get the range of the thing, and then it goes to your heart. Everything that stands athwart God's purpose is to be met with indignation, with uncompromising zeal, for this matter is so important. It is our loyalty to God. It is our oneness of heart with God's purpose.

God has a cherished purpose concerning His Son. In His infinite grace He has called us according to that purpose. The fact of what we are, as it breaks upon us so continually, is perhaps the thing which discourages us most of all from believing in a thing like this, and yet it is true that you and I, despite what we are, our utter worthlessness — ah, more than that, despite all the enmity that is in us against God by nature, all that is there that is so utterly contrary to God's nature, all the rebellion against God by nature, of which we are so capable under provocation — we are, by God's infinite grace, which comes down to us in Jesus Christ, called to govern the inhabited earth in the ages to come, for God, with God, in His Son. That is the purpose. That is what God is seeking in this dispensation, that instrument, that vessel for coming world-government.

When you and I recognize what the grace of God is, grace which finds a way for our forgiveness, and our deliverance from judgment, grace upon grace, ever mounting up until it sets us on the throne with Himself, in accordance with the word which He has spoken, "...shall sit with me in my throne, as I also overcame and am set down with my Father in his throne"; such grace coming home to our hearts surely would make us intensely jealous for God and deeply loyal to God. Surely if we felt that grace our attitude would be: "Oh, if anything dares to touch God's purpose, God's interest, that which is dearest of all to God's heart, I for one will have no compromise with that, I for one will show that I am utterly with God." That surely ought to be our reaction to the grace of God. It was because the apostle Paul had such a deep, deep sense of the grace of God in eternal purpose calling him that you find him so burning with zeal, so mightily stirred to white heat when there rose up something to interfere with God's purpose.

That explains the letter to the Galatians. Listen to his words in the first chapter. There is no compromise about this: "But though we, or an angel from heaven, should preach unto you any gospel other than that which we preached unto you, let him be anathema." That is very straight language. Let him be accursed. Why? Because he is interfering with God's purpose when he seeks to subvert the saints, when he interferes with their going on to full growth.

Sonship, adoption, is something which lies ahead. The adoption has not yet taken place. We are children of God, we have the Spirit of sonship, but the adoption is not yet; that is coming. The word "adoption" would help us more if it were translated literally; for it bears a different meaning in the New Testament from that which obtains among us today. The word simply means placing as sons, the installation as sons. It is rather the official element than the element of relationship. It occurs only five times in the New Testament, and these are all in Paul's letters, and every occurrence is very interesting and helpful.

So that is ahead, and it is that to which the apostle refers in his letter to the Romans: "The earnest expectation of the creation waiteth for the revealing of the sons of God." That lies in the future, and that is the day when the government of the inhabited earth to come will be taken up in the saints conformed to the image of His Son, in the church as mature.

Now you see, I am sure a little more of the importance, and why there is given such a place of importance to this matter of full growth. It is in maturity that the inheritance is to be possessed, that the placing of sons is to take place, that the subjecting of the inhabited earth to come is to transpire. Hence the need for going on to full growth. Government is important to God, and it is the full meaning of grace in the saints. So much, then, for our further emphasis upon the importance.

A Retrospect of the Letters to the Romans and Corinthians

We have said that these letters of the apostle Paul are each dealing with some aspect of spiritual maturity, or dealing with the matter from respective points of view. The letter to the Romans, as we have already pointed out, represents the work by which relatedness to the Lord is brought about unto His full purpose. The purpose is brought into view right at the outset, the manifestation of the sons of God conformed to the image of His Son. That is the purpose. Then everything is dealt with in order that a relationship shall be brought about, so that God can begin His purpose and proceed to its realization. Thus, in the letter to the Romans you have a revelation of God's attitude toward men by nature. The whole race is taken into view, and the verdict is, "All have sinned and fall short of the glory of God", and therefore lie under judgment and death. "There is none righteous, no, not one." Gentile and Jew are all in the same position before God. It is a startling fact, nevertheless clearly and positively stated; irreligious and religious; those who were without and those who were with the oracles of God. The natural difference that the oracles of God are seen to have made is that they have proved how helpless man is, and how deeply sinful he is by nature. The law came in, and, far from saving man, it only accentuated the natural condition of human weakness and sinfulness, and made manifest how impossible it is for man to stand up to God's requirement. So that universally man by nature is proved to be hopeless and helpless, under sin, condemnation, judgment and death.

Then the cross of the Lord Jesus is brought into view as the place where God's verdict concerning man universally was put into effect in the representative person of the Lord Jesus, who was made sin in our stead. The whole race passed under the actual judgment of God in the cross, and when Christ died, from God's standpoint, the race died under judgment.

Then the resurrection of the Lord Jesus comes in, as marking God's new beginning, a new relationship, where sin has been destroyed in judgment, and now, on the ground of sin having been destroyed and removed, there is a new relationship with God in Christ risen, in which relationship the Holy Spirit is given, the Spirit of the new creation. A new life is given — "...the law of the Spirit of life in Christ..." — and then in that new relationship, the purpose is embarked upon by the indwelling Spirit. Conformity to the image of His Son is the end. The call is that believers should apprehend that position of union with Christ in death, in burial, and resurrection, and by faith take their place therein. That becomes the foundation of God's purpose. Without that God cannot even make a beginning.

That is the letter to the Romans in brief. Our position by faith has to correspond to Jesus Christ crucified, dead, buried, risen and receiving the Holy Spirit, the Spirit of Sonship, to be led into God's purpose.

The first letter to the Corinthians takes us one step past that, and shows us the kind of person who will move on to God's end, to God's purpose, and what is necessary in believers in order that there may come about full spiritual growth. The key word in Romans is "in Christ": "There is therefore now no condemnation to them that are in Christ Jesus..." That is relationship. The key word to the first letter to the Corinthians is: "He that is spiritual..." The whole of that first letter has to do with spirituals in men and in things. The first letter to the Corinthians, then, has to do entirely with what a spiritual person is, how a spiritual person will act and speak; or, by contrast, how a spiritual person will not act and will not speak. The whole letter, chapter after chapter, sets carnality over against spirituality, and says, "Now this is carnality, and it blocks the way to God's end, and is the cause of spiritual arrest." It is necessary that a man shall be spiritual in the innermost reality of his being, that he shall be spiritually minded, and that this spiritual mind, the mind of Christ, shall govern him in every consideration.

One mark of the carnality of the Corinthians was their divisions, their natural preferences, likes and dislikes amongst people. Paul says, in effect, "If you were spiritual there would be none of that. If you are going on to full growth then you have to get clear of all that." So you go through the whole letter, and find that the finger of the Spirit lights through the apostle upon point after point, revealing carnality, and how it works out to spiritual arrest. They are seen to be full of contradictions, and full of denials, and full of limitation. He that is spiritual is not like that. Spirituality is essential to full growth.

In the second letter to the Corinthians the key word is "the face of Jesus Christ". By inference we are taken right back to the first creation. "God, who commanded the light to shine out of darkness..." (the first act in the creation), "...hath shined into our hearts to give the light of the knowledge of the glory of God in the face of Jesus Christ". What is the object of the creation? Jesus Christ is the object of the creation. Through Him, and unto Him, and by Him all things were created. But that object was not realized in the first creation, and whereas light came first, darkness soon followed on the disobedience of man, and so God's purpose in the face of Jesus Christ was not recognized; it was shut out. Now God begins His new creation: "If any man is in Christ, there is a new creation." What is the first thing that governs the new creation? "God... hath shined in our hearts, to give the light of the knowledge of the glory of God in the face of Jesus Christ." That is the key to everything.

How shall we reach God's purpose, God's end? How shall we grow in grace? By the continuous unveiling of God in Christ in our hearts. It has to go on, and so the word there heads up into this: "We… beholding (the word indicates continuous activity, maintaining our gaze, fixing our eyes) …are changed into the same image…" We are coming to God's end, the image of His Son, by the Holy Spirit keeping in our hearts a growing unveiling of the Lord Jesus.

We have the purpose of God set before us, we know what the calling is, we understand why we are urged to give diligence to make our calling and our election sure. We know that, while we may not fall from salvation, we may fall from the inheritance. We know that we may lose God's full purpose by not going on. Otherwise why this urge? We receive our salvation through grace, and I am quite sure that it will be the grace of God that carries us through unto the purpose; for who of us would get through, but by the grace of God? Nevertheless, for the inheritance unto the adoption as sons, coming to the government of the inhabited earth to come, there has to be an attitude of pressing on to full growth, lest we fail of the calling. It is the failure to recognize that which has led so many people into a fog, and into perplexity, and I think, into false teaching concerning certain things in the New Testament. It is the inheritance which governs. Until we are really governed by God's full purpose we do not understand a great deal of the New Testament. In the purpose of God we are "foreordained unto the adoption of sons by Jesus Christ", the placing as sons for governmental purposes in the ages to come.

Chapter 20

Christ Formed Within

Reading: Galatians 3.

"...I am again in travail until Christ be formed in you" Galatians *4:19.*

The Resistance to Divine Purpose

As we continue our meditation in relation to spiritual growth, spiritual full growth, recognizing, as we have sought to do, the very great and serious place which the matter occupies in the Word of God, and how important the Lord evidently regards it, there is the other side to that fact which must impress us, namely, the way in which this matter of spiritual growth is fraught with opposition. Whenever you touch upon it you find yourself in the presence of something set against it. It is never presented in passive conditions. It is always encompassed by active opposing elements and forces. You find that the exhortation, the encouragement, the admonition is all of the most positive character as over against something. Whenever God has moved in the past towards spiritual increase, there is always present some counter-move, some antagonistic element. You can see it through the Word of God again and again.

When the Lord would bring Israel from the bondage and limitation of Egypt, at once there was bitter conflict. When Israel was at last brought into the land, almost immediately there was an

Achan to arrest the whole movement and bring to a standstill that development unto the fullness of which the land spoke, and for the moment it was effectively done. So you may see it in a great number of instances in the Old Testament.

When God brought His Son into the world, which was a great movement towards spiritual fullness, there was to begin with a Herod, and then the Jews in their prejudice. Let us take note of the fact that prejudice is always set against spiritual progress. Prejudice never does give God a chance. It is a closed door. If one thing more than another marked the Jews, in the days when He who was God's fullness came amongst men, it was prejudice, and it was that which limited them, and robbed them of God's full purpose.

When the Day of Pentecost was fully come, and a mighty move towards fullness was made — that which the apostle later refers to as "the fullness of him that filleth all in all" — hardly has the church started upon its course before you find a suitable instrument to the enemy's arresting work in Ananias and Sapphira. Then you move on to the great apostle Paul, and always dogging his steps everywhere are the Judaisers.

So it is, that every movement of God is met by a counter-movement. Every step towards spiritual enlargement finds something present from the other side to check it, to arrest it, to frustrate it.

The Letters of Paul

Thus these letters of Paul bring up into view a large number of things which Satan has produced, very largely through the flesh, as counter-movements to God's end — full growth. As we have seen, in Corinth it was carnality, and also in Corinth, as is made perfectly clear in the early chapters of the second letter to the Corinthians, and among the Galatians, it was the Judaisers. Theirs was a very unworthy way of going to work. One of their great strokes against what God was seeking to do, was doing through His servant Paul, was their attack upon him in person; that is, their attack upon him as the vessel being used by God, an attack in ways unworthy of those who professed to be seeking the interests of God.

It is always so. When God moves and takes up a vessel for the increase of Christ in His people, for spiritual enlargement, Satan raises up an attack upon that vessel, and seeks to frustrate the purpose by prejudicing that purpose through the vessel in some way. He will misrepresent, lie — oh, he will use every kind of movement to discount the instrument, so that the divine object may fall into disrepute or be brought under arrest.

Now here is a letter (the letter to the Galatians) which is full of terrific conflict. Martin Luther was a fighter if he was anything, and he said he had betrothed this letter to himself. But what did Luther say further in relation to that? "Beforehand I was in quietness and comfort, in rest and acceptance, but since I have surrounded myself with a solid block of enemies"! That is significant because of what this letter stands for. Would to God that Martin Luther had seen all that it stands for, instead of only its beginnings. However, here we are in the presence of conflict, and the point is for us to recognize that if God is moving towards the enlargement of the measure of Christ in the saints, that movement encounters all hell's antagonism, and the vessel used by the Lord to that end will come under the massed assaults of the enemy, both vehement and malicious. He will stop short at nothing in seeking to render that vessel inoperative, to paralyze it, so that it cannot fulfill its divine mission. I always take the apostle Paul as a personal representative of the truth which was committed to him, as a vessel, one in whom all that related to that truth was wrought out in his own history; and in this point, as in so many others, it is quite manifest that Paul was raised up as a special vessel in relation to the full, eternal purpose of God concerning the church, and there was not another man in the dispensation who so met the force of hell, in its endeavor to paralyze and destroy, as that man. He stands to show us in his own history, and in his own person, what we may expect if we are linked with God's full purpose.

This should be enlightening and encouraging, looked at from one standpoint. It should explain things, and it should set us on our feet. The danger so often with us, when there is a mighty uprising of spiritual antagonism and we are made to suffer, and are suffering intensely, is that we should regard that suffering as something in itself, seek to attribute it to natural causes, to feel that it is something in the course of life which has come our way. We think we are just sufferers, and fail to see that, however the thing may appear to be like that, it is related definitely and directly to the purpose with which we are occupied.

It may be that you are not able to enter into this, because you are not in the experience of it, but others will understand. Believe me, that if you have betrothed God's full purpose to you, if you are married to God's full thought for His people — for yourself and for others, especially for the church — you are going to meet the Devil's attempted frustration of it in every conceivable way; the frustration of yourself, the frustration of your ministry. You are going to meet it physically, you are going to meet it in your soul, and you are going to meet it spiritually. You are going to meet it inside yourself, and you are going to meet it outside yourself. You are going to find yourself in a battle. And what is true of the individual will be true of any company that is standing in relation to God for that purpose.

The Form of the Attack among the Galatians

So we find ourselves in that very atmosphere immediately we open this letter to the Galatians. Paul wastes no time here. He uses very few words by way of nicety. He introduces himself, and his introduction is an attack. He opens the battle in his first sentence. "Paul, an apostle (not from men, neither through man...)" That is an attack. The battle is joined. Judaisers have been at work, and they have persuaded these Galatians that Paul was not an authentic apostle, but had set himself up as something; he was not one of the twelve, but was self-appointed. "Paul, an apostle (not from men, neither through man, but through Jesus Christ, and God the Father, who raised him from the dead)." You see, that is accepting the challenge. How it goes to the heart of things! It takes hold of the sword of the enemy and turns it right round and pierces himself. The Judaisers say I am not an apostle by recognition of Jerusalem; I have not been ordained at headquarters; I am not one of the authentic twelve; I have not received my credentials from the ecclesiastics, those who are called pillars. I agree! But I take my apostleship higher; I received it "through Jesus Christ, and God the Father..." What can you say to that? How are you going to handle that?

Now that is only just to point out that you are in the presence of conflict, and to establish the fact that where God is seeking to move towards the bringing of His Son to full formation in the church, Satan is always most active to defeat that end by any means possible. Bear that in mind at all times. The Lord help us to do it. If we remember that, it will be to our salvation.

What the Judaisers sought to do is perhaps something which we need not consider in detail. Had they had their way, this is what the effect and the outcome would have been, namely, that the Galatians would have returned to, and have become settled and fixed in religious formality, in ceremonial and ritual, in tradition and external religious works at the cost, firstly, of life, and ultimately of God's eternal purpose. The apostle takes up the battle for life in this letter, and makes it an issue of life.

We can clearly see that the method of the enemy was not restricted to the Galatians, for it had gone on before their day, and it goes on still: formalism, religious formality, ceremonial, ritual, religious traditions, many outward works in the name of God, all that in the place of, firstly, spiritual life, and then, finally, in the place of God's full intention for His people. That is very true. Of course, the enemy always knows where he has a salient point, where he has a vantage ground. These Galatians were mainly Gentiles, and they had come out of paganism, and in their pagan religious system there were many rites and ceremonials, many religious ordinances. There were all those performances and outward activities which constituted the form of worship of their gods, and to the natural man, the man of the soul, such things are indispensable. He must have what is tangible, he must have helps in religion; he must hear something, see something, do something, handle something. All these accompaniments of religion are essential to religion, and his religion would be a poor, starved thing if you took those away. Take the artistic away, take the aesthetic away, take away all the externals that come to our senses, and those means by which we express our sentient life, and what is religion? This pure, spiritual life of faith without anything of that is an uninteresting thing to the soul, and is very vague. Yes, what an unreal thing it is! These Galatians had come out of all that other thing, and had turned to the Lord. Then the Judaisers had come along with the Jewish order, and said, "Except you are circumcised you cannot be saved, and what you need is to come back to the Jewish ordinances". If you are at low ebb spiritually you are not able to stand up to that sort of thing very well, when there are plausible arguments and strong constraints, and when there is a turning upon the instrument which has been used for you and the pointing out of all the flaws and weaknesses in that one, and the showing of how that one has set himself up to be something which is contrary to the accepted position at Jerusalem. These leaders in Jerusalem had known Jesus Christ personally, in the flesh; they had been with Him, and they did not agree with this sort of thing, they still believed in these Jewish ordinances. "So you see Paul is all wrong; he is just one by himself, no one agrees with him", was what they urged.

It was all so subtle, and thus Satan had his point with them in relation to their old form of life, working on that uncrucified soul-life, and they came under the spell. "O, foolish Galatians, who hath bewitched you?" As we have pointed out, the literal words there are, "Who did cast over you the witch's spell?" A spell is a nice sensation, till you wake up. A spell is usually cast over a person in order to rob him of something, and that in fact is what happened in the case before us.

Spiritual Apprehension of Christ

Let us, then, recognize the point, namely, that in Christ we are called out of that whole thing. That is earthly, that is of man, tradition, religious system of rites and ordinances, of days, times and seasons. We have been called out of that into a heavenly life in Jesus Christ by faith. When you really do get through you never have any inclination towards that other thing again, you are spoiled for it. But that is just the point of Galatians 4:19: "My little children for whom I am again in travail until Christ be formed in you." Paul was not saying at this point that he was in travail in relation to that end when Christ should be fully formed in them in the purpose of God. Of course, it had its bearing upon that, it was related to that ultimately, but that is not what he means here; not that full conformity to the image of Christ, not that full development of Christ in them. What he is saying here is this: "I am in travail until Christ takes definite shape in you." It is the difference between the embryo and the fully formed child. He said he was in agony about that. The trouble with them was that they had not clearly seen Christ, not clearly apprehended Christ; Christ was not distinctly defined in them, the meaning of Christ had not become definite in them. Something had happened. They had been begotten from above, they had received the Spirit, by faith they had turned to the Lord Jesus, but it has become evident that they have not grasped the significance of Christ. Paul said, "I fear lest I have bestowed upon you labor in vain." What is labor in vain? Oh beloved, in relation to God's purpose, in relation to God's full thought, it is far from being enough that we should just believe on the Lord Jesus; it is essential that we should see who and what Jesus is, and what He means.

If you want proof that this is the point here between Paul and the Galatians, recognize this, that the personal name of the Lord Jesus

Christ occurs forty-three times in this very brief letter. It is not the descriptive title, as so often elsewhere. It is the personal name, the Man Christ Jesus thirty-nine times out of the forty-three in this letter. Why? Why should he bring such a tremendous number of references to Him into this letter? Well, it is self-evident. Hear his exclamation, to this effect: "Before whose eyes Jesus Christ was openly set forth, crucified", placarded openly, and you have not seen! Four times in this letter the Cross of Christ is referred to in relation to the biggest things with which we have to do. We are not going to stop now with them, but those four statements about the Cross of the Lord Jesus in this letter are the greatest things that could be said about the Cross, and they all have reference to the end of the personal ego: "I have been crucified..." — the all-embracing fact; then, by the same means, severance from the law — "I... died unto the law"; severance from the flesh — "They that are of Christ Jesus have crucified the flesh with the passions and the lusts thereof"; severance from the world — "Far be it from me to glory, save in the cross of our Lord Jesus Christ, through which the world hath been crucified unto me, and I unto the world." "Before whose eyes Jesus Christ was openly set forth crucified", and you have not seen the implications.

If you had but believed (Galatians and all others) you would have once for all been delivered from earthly religious systems, earthly orders, rites, ceremonies, traditions, and all that sort of thing, and you would be in a heavenly place; for Christ crucified means that. To apprehend Christ means absolute emancipation out of everything here, even in a religious way, after a religious kind. It is that which represents the whole question of maturity and immaturity. You ask, What was it that constituted immaturity amongst the Galatians? It was that, under persuasion, influence and argument, they were ready to drop back so easily and so quickly into an earthly religious order with which the Cross of Christ had finished, which the Cross of Christ had brought to an end. Oh yes, the law of Moses, and all his order, and his ritual ended in the Cross of the Lord Jesus. It served a purpose, but reached its fulfillment in Christ, and Christ crucified marked an end. In Christ risen, all that it pointed to is taken up in a spiritual way to heaven, and now we are united with Christ in heaven. He fulfills all the values of that for us. He is our High Priest, our sacrifice, our precious Blood, our meeting place, our righteousness, our approach, our access to God, our acceptance. Everything shadowed in the types and figures is carried up into Him risen and exalted, and we have it all in spiritual value. Yes, you say, but it is all so far away, and unreal, and we want something that we can handle and see and hear. Ah, that is immaturity, that is spiritual infancy. Children always want something (and rightly so) that they can see and hear. But the apostle in this letter plunges the Galatians right into the place where all those infant things are finished with. He says, "You must begin sonship from the beginning". It is remarkable how far advanced he is in his point of view in this letter.

While the placing of sons lies in the future, while the inheritance lies there, the apostle says, we are all sons of God by faith in Jesus Christ, and we are expected now to begin to live upon the sonship principle. We do not want toys to play with on the earth, picture books to look at, object lessons, but we have come in spirit immediately to an apprehension of Jesus Christ, and a living fellowship with Him, so that all that kind of thing is passed. The Cross of the Lord Jesus in this letter is not set forth merely in relation to what we would call gross sin, but is set over against all religion in the flesh, and when Paul says, "I have been crucified with Christ; yet I live; and yet no longer I, but Christ liveth in me", he further adds: "and that life which I now live in the flesh, I live in faith, the faith which is in the Son of God..." You notice the context. It is the difference between life in the law and life in the risen Christ; not the difference between the religious life of the Jew as such and the religious man as such. All that is one thing, and the Cross cuts that off, and the "I" that is in that is brought to an end. Now I live, he says, "yet no longer I, but Christ... and that life which I now live I live in faith, the faith which is in the Son of God..." It is a kind of life. The Cross brings out to that kind of life which is the life of the Son of God lived by us through faith. That must be reserved for further consideration. We will stay with the more obvious points in the letter.

Christ Formed Within, a Question of Supreme Importance

I think we can be content to dwell for a little while longer upon those words in chapter 4:19: "My little children, of whom I am again in travail until Christ be formed in you."

It is the anguished cry that believers should come to a place where they are fixed — "Christ be formed". It is the place where there is some definiteness in them as to the Lord Jesus. It is a settled thing. They have *SEEN* the Lord Jesus and they are settled. You cannot move them; that is, they have the root of the matter in themselves. Christ has taken shape in them.

Now, if Paul agonizes, groans, travails in that connection, how important it is, and what serious consequences must be related to a Galatian condition. The crying need amongst the Lord's people is that they should come to a fixed and settled place and position in consequence of the meaning of Christ having come home to them in clearness and in definiteness; that they should be settled and grounded, not easily moved away, not easily falling under the witch's spell. They know the Lord, and you cannot move them. You do not have to nurse people like that. You do not have to keep picking them up and putting them on their feet. You have to supply no crutches. You can count on them. You know that they have that basic knowledge of the Lord, that they will not be moved away easily, that they will go right on. They see what this means; they have grasped the significance of Jesus Christ, and you can count on them to go on. You will agree that this is a very necessary state to God's end, which is full growth; to have an initial and fundamental grasp of the significance of Christ, and to have become fixed in relation to Him. It is because that is lacking that there is such spiritual poverty and limitation, weakness, defectiveness and defeat everywhere. It is a matter of seeing the Lord Jesus.

That is why the apostle uses, with all his might, his own personal experience as a case in point. He opens this letter, and takes up the battle. He declares his apostleship as from heaven, and not from men. Then he goes on with his own case, and before long he will say, "It pleased God, who separated me from my mother's womb, and called me by his grace, to reveal his Son in me." When that happened, he says, in effect, "I went not up to confer with flesh and blood at Jerusalem; I had the root of the matter in myself by direct act of the Holy Spirit."

All is by the Spirit

Go through this letter again and count the number of times that the Spirit is mentioned. You will find everywhere it is the Spirit, and it is this inward work of the Holy Spirit in the heart that makes him see the Lord Jesus. I am not talking about seeing a figure, not about seeing a person as such; I am talking about seeing the meaning of God's Son, the meaning of the Man Christ Jesus, how He gathers up everything that has ever been, or ever will be, in His own person, and becomes the embodiment of all God's thought, intention, and the fountain-head of every resource in relation to that purpose of God: and He becomes that to him. Paul needs no Jewish altars, no Jewish priests, no Jewish blood-shedding and sacrifices, no Jewish temple or tabernacle. Jesus Christ is all that and infinitely more to him. Paul does not live by those things, Jesus Christ is his life. He does not need guidance from those things, Jesus Christ is his guidance. It is what the Lord Jesus is to him that is the sum total of it all.

When you have that, you are out, you are free. Oh, no one need say to you, You must do this, and you must not do that. That is the law. You are out, you are free, you have no life in that; you have rest, and liberty, and power, and peace in Christ, in communion with Him, in fellowship with God in Him. Think of the terrific fall this was on the part of the Galatians. Paul appeals to them: "Oh you, who began in the Spirit, do you think now you can be perfected in the flesh? You who came into the way of all that by the Holy Spirit, do you think you are going to reach God's full end, be made perfect by coming down to fleshly religious activities? It is unthinkable. No wonder you find Paul amazed, perplexed, bewildered and vehemently angry that anybody would so undo the Cross of Christ, so set aside the life in the Spirit. Spiritual maturity is that the Holy Spirit has revealed and is revealing all the meaning of CHRIST IN US, and we are living on Him. Spiritual immaturity is that we must have all these external religious things to help us to be good, and with a very unsatisfactory result. Do you see the point? Read the letter again in the light of this word: "Because ye are sons, God sent forth the Spirit of his Son into our hearts, crying, Abba..." In the original languages of the Bible, the Hebrew and the Greek, when you read that particular clause you are using exactly the word that the Lord Jesus used when He prayed to the Father. When He prayed He did not say in English, Father! He said, "Abba"! I do not see any particular value in it coming down to us like that, but it is strange that the Holy Spirit has preserved that, and given us the original word and then the translation, as though He would bring us right into the closest touch with this thing, bring us there in spirit to the very heart of the Lord Jesus.

Just as Jesus Christ said to the Father, Abba! so the same Spirit as in Christ is in us causing us to know the same relationship with the Father as He had: "Because ye are sons, God sent forth the Spirit of his Son into our hearts, crying, Abba..." That is where life in the Spirit begins — Father! It is by the Spirit of His Son.

You see God's purpose, God's end, that we should be conformed to the image of His Son. The Spirit of His Son in us crying "Father", revealing Christ in us. "It pleased God... to reveal his Son in me." That puts everything on the inside from start to finish, the beginning and the end; the first step and the fullness is bound up with that. "Reveal his Son in me"! That stands over against all externalities of religion. The difference is between life and death, earth and heaven, time and eternity. And so Paul calls this liberty, "the liberty of the sons of God." "Stand fast therefore in the liberty…"

May the Lord make this all clear, and bring it home to our hearts, that we may know Christ.

Chapter 21

The Unveiling of Jesus Christ in the Heart

Reading: Galatians 3; 5:13.

Paul was continually growing in the knowledge of Jesus Christ, but it was a comprehensive knowledge or revelation which took him immediately away into Arabia for an extended period, that he might be occupied with its implications, and when he came back it is quite clear he had grasped the significance of that revelation; he had seen what Jesus meant in God's thought. One of the things that had happened was that, with that revelation, he had gone back over the whole of the history of the people with whom he was joined by birth, right back over Jewish history, right back over his own relationship with Judaism, and he had seen very clearly that the Lord Jesus was the center of all that in the thought of God, that He took up all the spiritual values into His own person, and that Judaism as a religious system, traditional, historical, no longer obtained in the thought of God, but that what did exist in the place of it was Jesus Christ in heaven. All that Judaism meant which was of spiritual value was centered in a living person, and no longer to be had in a system, in a tradition, in an outward order of things, all of which was lifeless, ineffective, incapable of bringing about heart satisfaction and the realization of heart longing, deliverance from sin and the quietening forever of conscience. What Paul had now come to see was that all that to which Judaism pointed, but which it was incapable of realizing or fulfilling, was to be had and that he had it in the living, risen person, in Jesus Christ.

Liberty a Fruit of Revelation

That is only one thing which Paul saw, but that had a tremendous effect upon him. It did what nothing else in all this universe could have done. It absolutely delivered Saul of Tarsus, the rabid, vehement Jew, from his Judaism. It emancipated him from the whole of that system as an earthly system, although it had been given of God for a purpose. Nothing could have delivered Saul of Tarsus from that but a revelation of Jesus Christ. It is always futile and dangerous to advise people to leave one thing until they have a revelation of the fuller, and only such a revelation will accomplish the true emancipation. The word liberty and similar terms in this letter is what is meant by that. It is the absolute emancipation from the limitation, the bondage and the tyranny of an earthly religious system which constantly says, Thou shalt! and, Thou shalt not! You must! and, You must not! bringing under the hammer of law all the time. This deliverance emancipates completely from that into glorious liberty, in which you may do exactly as you like, because your lives are all lifted into the heavenlies.

In so saying let us be careful, because there are those who take cover under grace, under emancipation from law, for doing the desires of the flesh. There are many people who serve their own pleasure on the Lord's day, and argue that they are not under law but under grace. Be careful, because Paul says here, "For ye, brethren, were called unto liberty; only use not your liberty for an occasion to the flesh." If you do that, remember you are undoing the work of the Cross of the Lord Jesus, and are violating the work of the Holy Spirit, and are not at all in the realm of grace as set forth here. So let us not think that because we are not under the law of the Sabbath day in which we are forbidden to do a lot of things we can just do as the flesh likes; for the difference here is between the flesh and the Spirit. It is not a new bondage, but a new liberty, the liberty of an entirely new power of life and direction in life.

Paul says that his emancipation, the effecting of that glorious deliverance, was by the inward revelation of Jesus Christ. That is where we begin in our spiritual maturity. We must come there. That is rest. People who are still under law, even though it be Christian law, hedged up by, Thou shalt! and, Thou shalt not! are people who are usually very limited in their spiritual capacity, in their spiritual measure. Those who have really seen by revelation of the Holy Spirit what Jesus Christ is, have been set free, and have been put in the way of a great capacity for spiritual enlargement. They are at rest, and rest is a basic factor for spiritual growth. There is nothing which limits and defeats increase like unrest. That is a law in the physical realm. If in the physical realm you are without rest, then you do not make progress, you do not grow, you do not develop. It is those carefree people who arrive at the large physical proportions in the natural realm. It is like that in the spiritual realm with regard to our spiritual life, that it grows apace once there is basic rest. The law is a distressing thing, a wearying thing, a fretting thing. Whatever the law is, whether Jewish or Christian, it is an irritating thing, saying, You must do this! and, You must not do that! The Lord would have us to be stripped of that, and not be brought under that yoke of bondage as His children, but be living in the enjoyment of the Lord Jesus. We shall not do less because of that. We shall not refrain on that ground from many things which we do by compulsion. The matter of going to the gatherings of the Lord's people may serve us as an illustration here. You can go legally, or you can go in liberty. You can go because you are expected to, because people will wonder if you are not there, and the Lord will be grieved if you do not go. That kind of constraint is legal, and the Lord, if you only knew it, does not want you to gather on that ground at all. You will not gain very much if you do. It will all become a great burden, and you will be wishing there were not so many meetings. If, however, you are living in the enjoyment of the Lord Jesus you will not put in fewer meetings; you will be there, but you will be there in life, in enjoyment; you will be there unto gain, unto real good. That is liberty.

I simply take that as an example, by way of illustration. It applies to everything else. If you are really living in the enjoyment of the Lord, no one will have to say to you, You must not do that! Were they to do so you would reply, "I do not want to, I have no interest in that, I have something better." Liberty is the transcendence of the Lord Jesus, the infinite realm into which we have come, the greater, the heavenly, the more glorious, and we are out of all the other.

That is exactly what happened with Paul in this great matter of deliverance from Judaism. He saw what those Judaisers were doing, that those who had been led to Christ through his instrumentality were simply being brought down out of that glorious realm of liberty and fullness in Christ, on to the old legal basis again, that the Judaisers were destroying all the work that Christ had done for their emancipation. They were in fact setting Christ aside. So Paul brings Christ into full view again and makes this the issue — and it is a tremendous thing, it is the old issue, it is the continuous issue — Christ or law, Christ or Judaism, Christ or merely traditional, historic religion; the living Person or the system.

Now, he says, I was delivered from all that burden and nothing but that revelation of Jesus Christ would have delivered me. He goes on in this letter to speak of his life in the Jews' religion. He waxed zealous above those of his own age, more exceeding zealous. He was a devotee of Judaism, and he would go all lengths for that system of things. Nothing would have changed him, but he saw Jesus Christ. God revealed His Son in him, and that brought it to pass.

It may not be applicable to many of us, but the principle is what I want you to recognize. You may not need to be emancipated from anything like Judaism or legalism, but the principle is this, that for all increase, progress, enlargement, growth, maturity, it is essential that there should be in the heart a continuous unveiling of Jesus

Christ, and you and I will never get to the end of that unveiling. It is possible for some of us to say with truth that this year we have seen more of the meaning of the Lord Jesus than in all the previous years of our lives. Can you say that? It is the most blessed and most wonderful thing to be able to recognize that there is a growing revelation of Jesus Christ within; you see more and more of what He means from God's standpoint, and as that is so, there comes this increase of the Lord Jesus, this increase to which this letter moves towards its close, the fruit of the Spirit, love. An increase of the revelation of Jesus Christ in the heart is an increase of the love of the Lord Jesus, the fruit of the Spirit. You are conscious that your heart is coming more and more under the constraint of His love, and that unloveliness is becoming subordinate to His love. There is more joy in the Lord Jesus today than ever, because you are seeing more of what He is. It is practical. That is spiritual growth: "It pleased God… to reveal his Son in me…"

The Relationship of Revelation to Falling Away

Let us lay the emphasis upon that principle as we pass on, the necessity that every one of us should have a personal and individual revelation of the living Christ by the Holy Spirit in our hearts. If we do not have that, then we shall be a prey to anything else that comes along. These Galatians fell a prey to the Judaisers, and I see so many of the Lord's people who have fallen a prey to some doctrine, to some theory, to something which is altogether a sideline. Whether it be truth, or not, is not the point, but people get carried away by universalism, for instance, or British Israelism, and become absorbed in these things. In some of these there is no truth at all; in most there is sufficient truth to make them a positive deception. But even supposing they were entirely true, the point is: Are they leading straight to God's end or are they something just up in a corner to hold us away from reaching that end? These Galatians became locked up in a side-issue of theories, of teaching, and they were not going on towards God's end.

How did that come about? An answer which is more often true than not is this, that they got into a low spiritual condition. There was not a continuance of inward, living seeing of the Lord Jesus. They had grasped Christianity at its beginnings, but Christ was not formed in them in this sense of taking shape, and because they were in such a position, with Christ not formed, not taking clear shape, not clearly defined and apprehended in the Spirit, these other things came along and captured them, sidetracked them, and now there they are in these little side-interests and you cannot touch them. That thing is everything to them, and it has kept them back from God's full purpose.

Revelation must be Continuous and Progressive

It is so important that there should be this continual, living unveiling of Christ in the heart if we are to reach God's full end.

Paul came to that revelation right at the beginning. It was initial, but also a directive revelation continuously. It was the basis of the direction of his life. "When it pleased God... to reveal his Son in me... immediately I conferred not with flesh and blood, neither went I up to Jerusalem to them which were apostles before me..." Why did he not do that? If he had accepted a system of teaching he would have gone and discussed it with other people who were interested, and who were in that system of teaching, to see if he had grasped it aright. He would have compared notes and said: "Now, look here, I have accepted this teaching; you are interested in it, and I want to know whether I have been right in my understanding of this teaching." Is this what it means? That would be conferring with flesh and blood. He would have sought out the authorities at headquarters on the matter. But no, "I conferred not with flesh and blood, neither went I up to Jerusalem to them which were apostles before me..." If you follow this letter through, you will find that here is a movement which is not a wrong kind of independence, but is the true movement of a personal knowledge of the Lord Jesus. It is directive throughout his life. He speaks of going up by revelation of Jesus Christ; a revelation of Jesus Christ was given to direct his movements. Mark you, it was not a revelation which took the form of a dictation: Paul, you go here, you go there, you go somewhere else. It was a revelation of a Person.

You may find difficulty in understanding that, but if the Lord should open our understanding on that matter we should see that all the movements of the Spirit of God are in some way bound up with the person of the Lord Jesus. They are an expression of Christ in some way. He is continuing His doing, and His speaking, He is going on with His work to the end of the dispensation. He has not abandoned the field, not left the scene of activities and withdrawn, and given it to us to go on; He is going on. He is the chief worker, the one who has all in His hands. But what He has in His hands is not a multitude of things that He is doing, it is an expression of Himself in some way. The Lord Jesus is putting Himself into things, and bringing things into relation with Himself. You look to the end of God, and you find that universally Jesus Christ is to be expressed in a spiritual way. What He is will at some future time fill this universe, and you need to know what the Lord Jesus is in order to have your life directed. You need to be governed by what He is; you need a revelation of Him.

We can take an illustration from the tabernacle in the wilderness. That tabernacle is a comprehensive expression in type of the person of Jesus Christ, and if we look at it at any point, whether of its constitution or of its operation, we see something of the Lord Jesus Christ. If we look at a pin of the tabernacle, we shall see something of Him expressed. So that the tabernacle becomes a great spiritual system, and Christ is that. Christ is not only a person, Christ is, in effect, in outworking, a great heavenly, spiritual system. When we come into Christ we come into a heavenly order. That is not some manual of instructions but a living person. If the Holy Spirit gets a real hold upon you and me, so that we are moving by the Holy Spirit, all our movements, on the one hand, will in some way be an expression of Christ, and, on the other hand, a bringing of things into relation to Christ, so that Christ becomes raised up in them. The question is not, Shall I go here? Shall I go there? Shall I do this, or shall I do that? The question is, Is Christ going to express Himself in some way? Is He going there? Is He going to manifest Himself there? Then I go with Him to be His instrument, His vessel. It is a matter of the person, not of a lot of things to be done.

That is a very difficult thing to explain, but Paul does make it clear that his life was governed by revelation of Jesus Christ. He went up by revelation of Jesus Christ. He recognized in the spirit that Christ was on the move in a certain direction, for a certain purpose. That was revealed to him, and so he moved by the Spirit because it was a case of the goings of Christ. That is how life is to be governed. Our prayer must not be, Lord, shall I do this, and shall I do the other? Shall I go here, or shall I go there? Our prayer is, Lord, art Thou going there? Art Thou going to do this or that? Dost Thou want me for Thy purpose here and there? It is all related to a living person. Otherwise you build up a great system of activities which we say are for Christ, instead of it being the direct, pure work of Christ. There is real value and meaning in that. It is a governing factor. What was initial in the life of the apostle was continuous; that is, his whole life from beginning to end was governed and actuated by a revelation of Jesus Christ.

A Position of Complete Dependence

It all amounted to this, that Christ had become everything for him. It was not a new religion, and it was not a new life work. It was not a new mission on the earth. If you have not got there already, you will, if you go on with the Lord long enough, come to the place where you do not want any more life-missions or work, or any more commissions; you will come to the place of such utter weakness and dependence and helplessness and self-emptiness that your whole attitude will be, Oh Lord, do save me from ever attempting anything unless Thou art going to do it. Lord, if Thou art not going to do that, then in mercy keep me from putting my hand to it. Paul was not out in some new enterprise; Paul was bound up with the person of Jesus Christ, and he says, "that life which I now live in the flesh I live in faith, the faith which is in the Son of God..." Christ and His life actuates the apostle. It is Christ's mission, Christ's purpose, not his. It is what the Lord is doing, and not what he is doing for the Lord. That is what it means; Christ becoming everything. So that for this we have no life apart from Christ, no strength, no wisdom, no knowledge; we have nothing, not even ability to live apart from Christ, to say nothing of ability to do; all natural energies and resources reduced by the sovereign act of the Lord, so that it shall be no longer I, but Christ, to live and to do.

That represents a position that is painful to us naturally, exceedingly painful. Even though we may sometimes come to the place where we say to the Lord: "Well, Lord, we are prepared to have infirmity and weakness and suffering if only it is made a background of Thy more exceeding power", we say, at the same time, "If it can be, deliver us from our infirmity." There is always a kickback from that utterance. Here is the man whom we are taking as a personal representation of the truth which came in through him. If ever there was one man who stood in the light of God's full purpose in this dispensation it was the apostle Paul. Here he is and he is saying very much about his infirmity, the weakness which was in his flesh. He tells these Galatians that because of the weakness and infirmity of his flesh they did not despise him; nay, that they would have plucked out their very eyes for him could they have done so; showing what that infirmity was, something which made him despicable. I think there is a close resemblance between this statement and that in 2 Corinthians 12: "There was given to me a thorn in the flesh, a messenger of Satan to buffet me..." He says that it was given to him lest he should be exalted above measure. Here is a statement that the infirmity, the trial, the temptation that was in his flesh they despised not. At the close of his letter he said: "See with how large letters I write unto you with mine own hand." Now all that is the human background of this work of bringing the saints to maturity.

Maturity demands that there shall be ever a lessening of the human element, the natural element of the flesh, of our own strength, our own wisdom, our own competence, our own self-reliance. We must be brought down, so that we cry to God: "Do not allow us to be brought into things unless Thou art going to do them". When you get there, you are in the way of being a vessel unto the maturing of the saints. It is true that the more there is of us the less there will be of Christ through us to others; the less there is of us the more there can be of Christ through us to others. It is the way of maturity. That is what is meant by the revelation of Jesus Christ.

What is the nature of our revelation of Jesus Christ? We have found Him our strength in weakness; we have found Him our life in death; we have found Him our wisdom in difficulty, in problem, in mental defeat; we have found Him our rest in trouble, our joy in sorrow. We have found Him. It is the revelation of Jesus Christ to us by the Holy Spirit. That is the way of growth. That is the way of a ministry of growth. This is emancipation, this is liberty, this is life-union with the living person by revelation of the Holy Spirit. Paul shows that there are a good many other things which come out of this revelation. There is deliverance from the flesh along this line. You remember he cried, as recorded at the end of chapter 7 of his letter to the Romans: "O wretched man that I am; who shall deliver me from the body of this death?" Deliverance is through our Lord Jesus Christ: "I thank God through Jesus Christ our Lord." Now Paul says to these Galatians, "They that are Christ's have crucified the flesh, with the affections and lusts"; they are delivered from the flesh by revelation of Jesus Christ. "I thank God..."; I see the way out; it is through Jesus Christ. He sets this over against the law. How did they, under the law, hope to get deliverance from the flesh? By all kinds of rites, and ceremonies, and forms, and religious practices, and observances, by the "Thou shalt", and, "Thou shalt not"; and it never came. When the Holy Spirit reveals the Lord Jesus there is that deliverance. There is no spiritual growth and fullness until there is the deliverance from the bondage and tyranny of the flesh.

Now that requires a great deal more time than we can give to it at the moment, but we have so often said that if we really do see the Lord Jesus, the one in whom the whole question of sin was fought and finally defeated, and the power of the flesh was entirely overcome by the power of the Spirit; and we see Him because of the full, complete triumph which took place in Him over the flesh by the Spirit at God's right hand, there is a virtue in what He is there for us as victory over the flesh. We gather round the Lord's Table and eat and drink of symbols of His Body and His Blood. What does that mean? It is an act of faith that we take Him to be our life down here. This Blood is the incorruptible life of the Lord Jesus, sinless, deathless. It is for me down here now until my work is done, to maintain me in the midst of these conditions. There is a living Lord to minister to me, to maintain me against the working of infirmity until God has finished with the vessel. There is something in Jesus Christ for our deliverance now from the working of all the old creation.

Let us pray on the ground of His victorious humanity, and let us live on the basis of His victorious humanity; He is there for us. All the virtue of what He is in glory is to be ministered to us by the Holy Spirit now. By revelation of Jesus Christ we are delivered from the law, from the flesh, yes, from all things. If you do not understand that, nevertheless it is important and valuable. Ask the Lord to make it so for His glory.

Chapter 22

The Place and Work of the Holy Spirit

There is one line running right through this letter to the Galatians which seems to reveal perhaps the main factor in spiritual growth: the place and work of the Holy Spirit. We should do well if we were to follow that line through at this time. There are some thirteen references to the Holy Spirit in the letter. We shall not refer to them all, but confine ourselves to several quite distinct features or factors connected therewith.

It is quite clear from this letter, and, of course, from other parts of the Word, that the Holy Spirit is essential and basic to the realizing of all the purposes of God in the individual believer and in the church. It may help us to come to quite a simple presentation of that truth as it is unfolded in this letter.

The Receiving of the Spirit

In this connection read chapter 3:1-2: "O foolish Galatians, who did bewitch you, before whose eyes Jesus Christ was openly set forth crucified? This only would I learn from you, Received ye the Spirit by the works of the law, or by the hearing of faith?"

Those words in verse 2 touch the matter right at the beginning in the simplest, most elementary form. They have to do with the receiving of the Spirit. We must pause for a moment to recollect the connection between this interrogation and the whole purpose of the letter. It would seem that the apostle is doing something like this. He is saying, "Now you Galatians responded to the message of the gospel, and in doing so you made a tremendous move from one realm to another. You came right out of that whole pagan realm with its externalities of religious observance, all its practices. You forsook all, and you took the position of simple, definite faith in the Lord Jesus. When you did so, the seal of your acceptance, the seal upon your faith attitude, the mark which God gave that you were a new creation in Christ, was that you received the Holy Spirit; and you received the Holy Spirit from God, that all God's purpose in you should be realized, now that you had come into a living relationship with Him in His Son, Jesus Christ. That receiving of the Holy Spirit was basic and all-inclusive. It was the seal, the earnest, the guarantee. With the Holy Spirit you had the assurance of everything, you had the dynamic of everything; there was nothing more to be anxious about. Receiving the Spirit, the inheritance is secured unto you, you are sealed. It was a tremendous thing for you to receive the Holy Spirit, because it meant that God had started His work and had got the ground in you for carrying His work right through to completion. Yes, the Holy Spirit was everything for the purposes of God."

"How then did you receive the Spirit? You know quite well that you did not receive the Spirit by all your religious observances in paganism; they never got you through to that. It was when, upon hearing the message of the gospel concerning God's Son, you stepped out of that whole system of religious activities by a definite act of faith, and reposed your trust in the Lord Jesus. It was then that you received the Holy Spirit, 'not by works of law'." (You must drop out the article there. The margin corrects it. It is, "by works of law". There was the pagan law, just as there was the Mosaic law.) "It was not by works of law in your pagan religion that you received the Spirit, but by hearing the message of faith. It was a tremendous thing for you to receive the Holy Spirit; everything was included".

"Here are these Judaisers, coming along and telling you that you must observe the Mosaic law; that you must come back, not to your pagan law, but to Jewish law. To give heed to them is to be in danger of going back behind the Holy Spirit, back behind the gift of the Holy Spirit, back on to a ground which never issued in your receiving the Spirit".

Now that is the connection of the question. You can see how big a question it is, how much is involved. Thus the simple fact is the point for the moment. The receiving of the Holy Spirit includes all that God intends as to purpose, and power to realize that purpose; and all the light, and the guidance, and the knowledge, and the understanding, and everything that will bring about spiritual maturity unto God's end, is with the Holy Spirit. Receive the Spirit and you have all that in Him. It has to be worked out, but there it is. There is no work or effort of any kind whatsoever on our part bound up with our receiving the Holy Spirit. That is basic. We receive the Holy Spirit on exactly the same ground and basis as we receive justification, as we receive forgiveness, and that is by faith in the Lord Jesus, the hearing of faith, the message of faith. How did we receive forgiveness? We know that we never got forgiveness by struggling after it, or by working for it. How did we come into the blessed place of the justified? Never by any works of ours, but by faith in the grace of God. Not until we came to that position of simple, positive and definite faith in the grace of God in Jesus Christ did we receive forgiveness and justification. In exactly the same way we receive the Holy Spirit. That makes the beginning of this thing very simple: too simple for a great many people; too simple for this active, practical disposition of ours.

We do so often find ourselves in the attitude and position and state of mind that we must somehow do something in order to receive the Holy Spirit. Well, let us give heed to the apostle's challenge. The Holy Spirit is basic and all-inclusive for the purpose of God, you can have nothing greater. With the Holy Spirit you have everything, and all that on the simple, definite act of faith in the grace of God. We must remember that just as eternal life is spoken of as the gift of God to faith, so the Holy Spirit is also spoken of as the gift of God to faith. When you had forgiveness through the exercise of definite faith, did God give you instantly the witness that you had forgiveness, that you were a new creation? Were you not put to the test as to whether it was really faith or feeling? Were you not compelled to stand your ground very often without a sensation? "God for Christ's sake has forgiven you your sin, has justified you, has imputed unto you Christ's righteousness, has accepted you". Against a good deal of challenging you had to hold that ground. You found everything rising up to deny it, but faith called into operation became the ground of the ultimate assurance and the life which has issued therefrom, that you today know you are the Lord's. In exactly the same way the Holy Spirit is received, not in sensation, not in feeling, but in faith.

That is very elementary, but that is where the letter begins in this matter of the Holy Spirit, and you see what a lot is bound up with it. We have spent all this time in these meditations stressing the tremendous issue involved in that. How far-reaching this matter is! How heaven and hell are locked in a terrific conflict in relation to these souls, in relation to God's full purpose, and how the soul of the apostle is in travail because of the issues involved! Now right at the outset all that is brought to hang upon the simple yet definite receiving of the Holy Spirit. If you have truly recognized the ground upon which God gives the Holy Spirit you can never return to law, the law of carnal commandments contained in ordinances; you can never return to any ground of works; you can never return to any place where the externals of religion become the ground of your acceptance with God. It begins in faith, and it goes on in faith.

Let us recognize that everything begins with its beginning, everything hangs upon the first thing, and perhaps it is often necessary even for veterans in Christ to return to their beginnings. I am not sure that the next point does not find us out.

Continuing in the Spirit

"Are ye so foolish? having begun in the Spirit, are ye now perfected in the flesh?" (verse 3).

The margin renders it thus: "Do you now make an end in the flesh?" Having begun in the Spirit are you going to reach the end in the flesh? The apostle says quite clearly that the whole life has to be sustained and maintained by the Holy Spirit through faith, just as the beginning had to be made through faith in the Holy Spirit. The fact is that we do not change our position from one of abject need to one of personal ability when we become children of God. Having received the Spirit by faith, and having become the children of God, we are no more competent in ourselves to go on than we were to make a start. It is no more possible for us to reach the end now in ourselves than it was for us to make the beginning in ourselves. To change the basis at a subsequent point of time to the beginning will prove fatal. That is what happened here. The word to us, therefore, is that just as we made the beginning by the Spirit through faith, so shall we reach the end, and only so shall we reach the end; by the Spirit through faith. The Spirit has to do every bit of it, and we cannot do one fragment. Our only position is one of abiding faith in the Holy Spirit to carry it through to an end. But, seeing that, that is how it is done. There is not a fragment that God presents to us relative to all His full purpose but what the Holy Spirit given to us, is given for the purpose of making that real and actual, and not one fragment of it all can ever become real and actual apart from the Holy Spirit.

Now what is presented to you? A standard that is too high? Oh, that is far too high a standard, that is an ideal to which we can never attain, it is a life beyond us! It is all very wonderful, but it is not for simple folk like ourselves! Is that how you talk? Do you realize what you are doing? You are guilty, on the one hand, of unbelief, and you are setting at naught the Spirit of God. If God has set before us any goal, no matter how high, how great, how wonderful, then the gift of the Holy Spirit is to the end that we should reach that goal and not fail in one fragment of all the divine will and purpose. So our attitude should not be: "It is not too much for me; it is not too high, too great, too wonderful"; our attitude should be: "I have the Spirit, He can do it; I trust the Spirit implicitly to make it all good". We start in the Spirit and we go on in the Spirit; we cannot reach the end in the flesh. We can no more maintain our life than we can start it. It is with the Spirit.

The Spirit and Power for Service

"He therefore that supplieth to you the Spirit, and worketh miracles among you, doeth he it by the works of the law, or by the hearing of faith?" (Gal. 3:5).

The Revised Version margin says, "...doeth he it by works of law, or by the message of faith?" Here we come beyond the beginning of the Christian life, and beyond the question of the maintenance of the Christian life, to that of service, and of power for service. What is the basis? I think there is no more helpful way in which this could be put than the way in which it is put here: "He therefore that supplieth to you the Spirit, and worketh... among you". This, of course, refers to the Lord. The Lord supplies the Spirit to you, and works among you. It is the working power of the Holy Spirit in you and amongst you, that work of God, which is the evidence of His presence in service. He supplieth the Spirit: and in what way? How are we to find power for service? In what way shall we receive it? By nothing whatever that we can do. Oh, how many people are doing something to get power for service; doing lots of things very energetically, very patiently, with all the strength of their mind, in order that there may be the manifestation of God's power. They are making a tremendously strenuous business of it, and that is always a very dangerous thing to do. Here the apostle says that power in service is on exactly the same basis as the two previous questions we have dealt with, namely, that of the Holy Spirit as the seal of our acceptance, and of the Holy Spirit as the means of our maintenance. The Lord does not supply the Spirit in response to any energetic exercises of ours; He supplies the Spirit in response to faith, the same kind of faith as we exercised for our salvation, and as we are called upon to exercise in relation to reaching God's end.

The workings of the Spirit amongst us are gifts, and the Spirit is supplied through faith. Do you realize that? It will save us a lot of trouble, a lot of stress, and it may save us from a good many deceptions; for if there is one thing patent it is this, that a terrific soul-stress, soul-projecting, soul-concentration upon receiving power for service, is responded to by other powers, whose very vehicle of expression is our soul. We get the psychical in service, psychical powers and manifestations by other spirits, through this tremendous outgoing of soul-force in relation to power for service. It is a very dangerous thing. Perhaps we have touched something with which we should not go further, but it is a matter of much exercise of our hearts in these days to see how Satan is governing the world along that line. If you want the explanation of dictatorships it cannot be found in the natural realm. They are not men who are naturally capable of doing what they are doing. Their early life finds them as nonentities, something at a discount, and here they have come to be world factors with marvelous powers and phenomenal influence over the masses, so that they literally control and hold nations as slaves in their own hand. You look at their history and you find that it is the history of a projecting with unspeakable intensity of their own soul-force, providing the very platform upon which the powers of evil alight to carry out the work of Satan.

Now that is in the wide range, but you find this in what are called spiritual realms too. People begin to concentrate or project their souls upon spiritual things, and you get a manifestation of a false Holy Spirit, signs and wonders. It is psychical, and satanic through the psychical. The question of power is much simpler than that. "He that supplieth the Spirit and worketh miracles among you, doeth he it by the works of law, or by the hearing of faith?" Is your exercise and effort on the basis of what you do, or on the basis of faith? Power for service is on the basis of faith. It brings faith into a place of tremendous prominence and importance, but it shows that it is the Holy Spirit keeping things in His hands, and not putting them into our hands, not letting go to us. It is His work, not ours.

Let us cherish that little fragment, "He that ministereth (or, He that supplieth) the Spirit". It is the Lord who does it, and He does so in response to faith.

The Spirit and the Inheritance

"Christ redeemed us from the curse of the law, having become a curse for us: for it is written, Cursed is every one that hangeth on a tree: that upon the Gentiles might come the blessing of Abraham in Christ Jesus; that we might receive the promise of the Spirit through faith". (verses 13-14).

This is a very wonderful statement. The blessing of Abraham in Christ is for us. It is a tremendous thing that we who are Gentiles should receive in Christ this blessing. This promise has two parts to its fulfillment: firstly, They that are of faith are Abraham's seed. Christ is Abraham's seed. "He saith not, And to seeds, as of many; but as of one. And to thy seed, which is Christ." Thus faith makes us one with Christ as Abraham's seed to receive the covenant promise. The second part to its fulfillment is, "That we might receive the promise of the Spirit…" So that the Holy Spirit in the fullest sense is secured unto us in Abraham through faith. The receiving of the Spirit embraces all the promises in Christ; for, "How many soever be the promises of God, in him is the yea: wherefore also through him is the amen, unto the glory of God by us." How far-reaching this promise was to Abraham is hinted at in Romans 4:13: "For not through the law was the promise to Abraham or to his seed, that he should be heir of the world, but through the righteousness of faith".

How is the promise that he should be heir of the world to be fulfilled? In Christ. By what means? By the Holy Spirit. Thus in

Christ, by the Holy Spirit, we come into that which was first promised to Abraham, namely, the possession of the world. It is a wonderful thing. We are getting the purpose in view through the Holy Spirit. We are moving from beginnings, step by step. The progressiveness of things in this letter is remarkable. Here we come right in full view of the purpose: "heir of the world". The covenant was with Abraham; the covenant was fulfilled in Christ; the means by which the covenant is made good is the Holy Spirit, and we are the receivers of the Spirit. What, then, do we receive? The promise of heirship to the world, inheritance in the ages to come. Elsewhere the apostle speaks of the Holy Spirit as the earnest of our inheritance. "That he should be heir of the world"! How great a promise that is, and we are partakers of it.

How are we going to inherit the world? God has called us to that. How are we going to enter into it? By works of law, by efforts of our own, by our external activities of a religious kind? No, we must come back again to the simple foundation of faith. The Holy Spirit has come to bring us into that inheritance. The inhabited earth to come shall be placed under man according to God's mind, and that is the issue of the work of the Holy Spirit.

Oh, Lord, it is a great thought, too wonderful for us, that we should inherit the world, that we should reign over the earth, that we should be in governmental union with Christ in world dominion in the ages to come. Can it be? The Lord answers, I have given you the Holy Spirit, and He is the earnest of it. You put faith in Him, and He will bring it to pass.

World dominion is not such a strenuous thing, after all, as it is made out to be. It is a question of faith in the Holy Spirit. The Holy Spirit is the sum of all the promises, and all the blessings made and promised to Abraham.

The Witness of the Spirit

"And because ye are sons, God sent forth the Spirit of his Son into our hearts, crying, Abba, Father". (Galatians 4:6).

Here is the progressiveness in view again. We have seen the end, the inheritance. Who are they that inherit? Heirs. Who are heirs? Sons, firstborn sons. How are we constituted sons, and therefore heirs? He has sent forth His Spirit into our hearts, the Spirit of His Son who is the heir of all things. When the Holy Spirit constitutes that cry in our hearts, "Father", that very expression, as born in us of the Holy Spirit relates to the inheritance. It not only signifies that we are in the family, it relates to the inheritance. It is the Spirit of Sonship. This is not the Sonship of regeneration, but it is the Sonship of full union with Christ and all that this means.

Walking by the Spirit

"But I say, Walk by the Spirit, and ye shall not fulfill the lust of the flesh." (Gal. 5:16).

You see how all this is linked with spiritual maturity, full growth. Here is the whole secret of sanctification. They say, Face your besetments manfully, and wrestle with them courageously, and set yourself not to be beaten by them, but to master them! What poor advice, what tragedy is linked with such a course. It is much simpler than that. "Walk by the Spirit, and ye shall not fulfill the lust of the flesh". Oh, to give men something stronger! Yes, all right, here is something stronger: "For the flesh lusteth against the Spirit, and the Spirit against the flesh; for these are contrary the one to the other; that ye may not do the things that ye would." (verse 17). It just amounts to the question of who is the stronger, the Spirit of God or the flesh. Yes, the flesh lusteth against the Spirit. Is that a hopeful prospect for the flesh? No, for the Spirit is dead-set against the flesh, and working against it.

How does this work out to victory? The Spirit lusts against the flesh. You walk in the Spirit. What is it to walk in the Spirit? You take sides with the Holy Spirit, you cooperate with the Spirit, you let your exercise be in relation to the Holy Spirit, and you shall not fulfill the lusts of the flesh. The Spirit will get the upper hand of the lusts of the flesh as you take sides with Him; not as you struggle and fight against the lusts of the flesh, but as you cooperate with Him. It is only when you and I lean towards the flesh and take sides with it that we fail. There is present an energy and a power, and if we will deliberately take our place with that energy, that power, that person, there will be deliverance. It would be a hopeless thing otherwise, but that is the secret of sanctification, and that is the way of spiritual full-growth. The bringing in of the Holy Spirit there makes such a big difference. "For the flesh lusteth against the Spirit, and the Spirit against the flesh..." I have an idea that instead of "and" the word should be "but". If that is true it makes a lot of difference. It puts hope into the whole. Whether the word is there like that or not, the fact remains.

The Fruit of the Spirit

"But the fruit of the Spirit is love, joy, peace, longsuffering, kindness, goodness, faithfulness, meekness, self-control: against such there is no law." (Gal. 5:22-23).

The peculiar form of those words must be noted. "The fruit (that is singular) of the Spirit is (then you get plurality)..." The correct grammatical form would be, The fruits of the Spirit are — The fruit of the Spirit is love, and love comprehends all the rest, and all the rest are love in expression in different forms. You can test that. If you really have the love of God in your heart, what do you have? You have joy, love exulting; peace, love trusting; longsuffering, love enduring; gentleness, the refinement of love; meekness, love, as someone has said, with a bowed head; goodness, love in action; temperance, love in restraint; faith, love confiding.

All these things are included in love. The fruit of the Spirit is love. If you want to know what love is, it is all there. This is the outworking of the Holy Spirit. Has this anything to do with maturity, faith, growth? Of course it has. Spiritual maturity comes by the Holy Spirit bearing His fruit in us. The fruit of love working out in joy, peace, longsuffering, gentleness, meekness, goodness, temperance, faith.

Persevering in the Spirit

"If we live by the Spirit, by the Spirit let us also walk". (Gal. 5:25).

This is our voluntary and continual relationship with the Spirit actively. If we live by the Spirit — and from beginning to end it is all by the Spirit — then let us also walk by the Spirit. It is a voluntary handing over to the Holy Spirit and going on with Him continually. After all, we have everything by the Spirit from start to finish. Seeing that it is so, let us go on with the Spirit. But notice, it is not a passive life, it is an active life, an exercised walk. The point is the Spirit seeks that we shall be of moral and spiritual character. It is not a question of His taking it all out of our hands, doing it all apart from us, so that we simply recline and say, "Well, we have the Spirit and we need not do or think anything about it, it is all going to be done for us". Everything truly is by the Spirit in our life, but let us be active, not passive; let us walk by the Spirit. He is seeking to produce spiritual character, and that can only be through exercise, and our exercise must be towards the Holy Spirit, and as that is so we shall come to God's end, full growth.

Chapter 23

The Cross and Conformity to Christ

Reading: Romans 6.

"What we in glory soon shall be, It doth not yet appear; But when our blessed Lord we see, We shall His image bear." *["Behold, What Love" by M.S. Sullivan]*

The words upon which we have based our meditations correspond with those words. "The earnest expectation of the creation waiteth for the manifestation of the sons of God"; "Conformed to the image of his Son"; "We shall His image bear". We have covered a great deal of ground in connection with divine thought and purpose, passing through four of the letters of the apostle Paul.

In all of those letters there is one note struck upon which we have not dwelt particularly, although we have mentioned it from time to time, and it is that of the cross of Christ; and to go on from this time without recognising the place of the cross, in relation to God's purpose of conforming us to the image of His Son, would be to make the greatest of mistakes and to leave out the most fundamental thing. We will, therefore, briefly consider its place in these four letters of the apostle Paul, from Romans to Galatians. That does not mean that we are going to deal with every reference to the cross in each letter, but rather with the place given to it and its specific connection in each letter.

The Cross in Relation to Sin

It is quite clear that the place of the cross in the letter to the Romans is its relation to the whole question of sin, and until that matter is settled there is no prospect whatever of conformity to the image of God's Son. Now the terms used here make it abundantly plain that it is a matter which is settled once for all. It is something that is done at the beginning. But let us hasten to point out that it is not sins that are being dealt with. Sins are not the subject, but sin.

Leading up to this chapter the whole question of sin and righteousness has been under review, and there has been a search through the universe for righteousness in man as man's nature. That search has extended through the whole pagan world, and then to the whole Jewish world, and when all the ground of Jew and Gentile has been surveyed the verdict is that, not only is man not righteous, but that he is unrighteous by nature. "There is none righteous, no not one". So that all men are by nature included under unrighteousness. There is, therefore, no foundation upon which God can build His purpose; for God must have a foundation suited to that purpose. If it is His purpose that the image of His Son should be reproduced in men and women, in a creation, then the foundation thing surely must be righteousness; for that is where you begin with the character of Jesus Christ, the nature of Christ. It is a matter of righteousness. How, then, shall God provide Himself with an essential basis without which He is defeated in His purpose? God sent His Son in the likeness of sinful flesh, and, related thus to the unrighteous race, He was made sin. He took the unrighteous nature of man upon Him in His cross, in a representative way, although in Himself there was no sin. But as the substitute and representative of a race that is condemned, judged and lying under death, He, as a racial, inclusive representative, died under the hand of divine judgment, and in Him the race was caused to die from God's standpoint. That is how God views it. In Him sin is dealt with, unrighteousness is put away. In His resurrection He was "raised from the dead by the glory of the

Father". There is no glory except where there is righteousness. In His resurrection you have a representative righteous one, as in His death you have a representative unrighteous one. In His death He is offered a substitute for the sinner; in His resurrection He is presented a substitute for the believer, for the saint. Now the challenge is, Who is righteous?

The whole of the argument in this letter to the Romans, as you know, has to do with that righteousness which is by faith in Jesus Christ. That is, as to whether, on the one hand, we will exercise faith toward Jesus Christ as our substitute in death, in judgment, under the hand of God for destruction, and will lay our hands upon His head in faith and say, That is for me, for my sin, that is my judgment, my death; and on the other hand, as to whether, viewing Him as risen, with sin all done away, we will by faith lay our hands upon His head and say, This Righteous One is accepted for me, this one is my representative before God, His righteousness is mine. That is exercising faith in Jesus Christ and God accounts His righteousness ours, places it to our credit, and so the sin question is done away in the death and burial of the Lord Jesus. As we identify ourselves by faith with Him in death and burial, we are found where the whole body of sin is done away, and then, as by faith we identify ourselves with Him in resurrection, the whole body of righteousness abounds, and we are accounted righteous by God.

That is the simple element of the gospel. You are familiar with that, but that is where God begins, and that is the foundation. In the cross the whole body of sin, that which was interfering with God in the realisation of His purpose, is put away from God's sight. God Himself has put it away, and God has brought in righteousness by the resurrection of Jesus Christ from the dead, and in that way provided Himself with the ground upon which to take up His work, His purpose of conforming believers to the image of His Son.

It is important, then, for us to recognize that the whole sin question was settled, the whole body of sin was done away in Jesus Christ, and by faith accept that position, as also that the whole body of righteousness in Jesus Christ has been brought into view with God in resurrection, and that this is for such as will believe. We are accounted righteous before God by faith in Jesus Christ. Until that is settled we can get nowhere. While we have questions about that, God cannot go on with the conforming. That is why we said the question at issue is not that of sins but sin. We shall find, after that we have reached settlement on the matter, that there are elements of that old creation still about us, but that now God begins upon the basis of righteousness to deal with those, to conform us to the image of His Son, so that righteousness overcomes unrighteousness, and the nature of the Lord Jesus overcomes the old nature. But the essential beginning of God's operations is that we accept the whole as already accomplished in His Son, Jesus Christ. It is as though God were taking from the full and the final store which is in the person of His Son and making that good for us as we exercise faith in Him.

We need not say more about the letter to the Romans. It may be that some have not yet got past Romans 6. Well, the call is very clear, the position is unmistakable. The apostle says that this position can be taken in faith, and baptism is the way in which testimony is borne to the fact that we have taken that position. In our baptism we took the position of declaring that we were planted together with Him in His death, and are also united with Him in the likeness of His resurrection. That is where we begin. We have righteousness to begin with, God's essential foundation. If ever you get back behind that you arrest the work of God. If ever you have questions again about your standing before God on the basis of divine righteousness, you at once put God's hand from you in the conforming of you to the image of His Son, but while you take that position of faith, God's hand can do it. Do not argue about it; do not have all sorts of questions about it; do not allow the mere psychological elements to come into it, which say, "Well, is this trying to make ourselves believe something, an endeavour to take a position which is not actual and real?" Because we mentally take that position it is as a kind of subjective fact in us. Do not allow all that realm to come in, for it will certainly do so if you allow it. If you will positively and definitely reckon yourself, with regard to the sinful body of the flesh, to have been taken to death in the person of Christ, and if you will positively and definitely by faith reckon Christ's righteousness as yours, then God says, I will make that good to you, and will go on working in you towards My full end. You do the reckoning, and I will do the working, God says. You operate in faith, and I will operate in work. Thus God works on the basis of a settled thing in our hearts through faith. It is possible that we shall meet everything that can counter this possibly, as did Luther, the great exponent of this very truth of the letter to the Romans. He was continuously pursued by the enemy, who sought to bring him again under accusation and condemnation, but he always cleared himself by a strong and positive affirmation, right in the very face of Satan, that in Christ no sin was attributed to him; he was righteous. Thus it was he found the victory. That is to be our position; not to argue with the devil but to tell him the truth: and this is the truth, that in Christ we are by God regarded as sinless. We must honour Christ as our representative.

The Cross and the Natural Man

We pass from Romans to the first letter to the Corinthians, and here in chapter 2 verse 2 we have our reference to the cross: "For I determined not to know anything among you, save Jesus Christ, and him crucified".

That is a definite resolution, a determination. When Paul says a thing like that, he has made up his mind to take a certain position, and we may be sure that he has very good reason for doing it. The reason is perfectly patent as you read this letter. Here were believers in the Lord Jesus, Christians, who were nevertheless bringing into their Christian life all the elements of nature. These elements are very many, as the letter discloses. They are seeking to live in relation to the Lord Jesus on a basis of natural life, natural wisdom (that is the subject of chapters 2 and 3), natural strength; nature's preferences, nature's likes and nature's dislikes. The apostle does not say that they are unregenerate. He calls them the Lord's people, but he says of them that they are carnal; that is, fleshly Christians. They talk as men naturally talk. They think as men naturally think. They desire and choose, and select as do men naturally, and in every way they are doing what men do by nature. He sets that over against what men think, and say, and do, and feel, and desire, and select when spiritual. So he sets two men in opposition here, the natural man and the spiritual man. The one he calls the man of soul, the man of nature; the other he calls the man of spirit, the spiritual man. The word used for the latter is a very interesting word when you break it up — "pneumatikos" man. "Eikos" is likeness, form; an icon is a form, a likeness, an image. "Pneuma" is spirit. So that the word you have when you piece it together is "formed after the spirit", or "made suitable to what is spiritual". The other man is formed after nature, after the soul. Now that is why Paul determined not to know anything amongst them that was merely natural knowledge. That is to say, he was not coming down to their level, that everything should be known by natural ways on a natural basis. He saw that this was ruining the interests of the Lord in their life and destroying their testimony. Ah, but he knew this, that the cross of the Lord Jesus had not only dealt with the whole sin problem, but also with the whole problem of man himself. The natural-man question was settled as well as the sin question. In the death of the Lord Jesus, not only had man died as a sinner, but he had died as a man, a kind of being, a sort of creature who thinks like this, who speaks like this, who feels like this, who likes like this, who chooses like this. It is all according to nature, and in the cross of the Lord Jesus that man died, and in the resurrection of Jesus Christ another man, a man of spirit is brought in, who is spiritually minded, who thinks and desires and feels, not as natural men do, but as the Lord Jesus does: one who has the mind of Christ, who has the sensibilities of Christ, who has the inclinations of Christ, who has the tastes of Christ; and all that is so opposed to what you have here at Corinth.

The cross of the Lord Jesus, then, brings an end to a kind of man, namely, the natural man, and makes way for another man, a spiritual man. If you have any difficulties about that term "spiritual man" just remember the word means "one formed suitably to things spiritual". If you want to know what that is read on here: "Now the natural man receiveth not the things of the Spirit of God... he cannot know them, because they are spiritually judged. But he that is spiritual judgeth all things..." (1 Cor. 2:14-15). That is a man who is so constituted that by new divine faculties he is now capable of understanding divine things, and having communion with divine things, and living according to divine things. He is constituted, formed for that which is of God. The cross of the Lord Jesus cleaves between those two kinds of men. On the one hand it brings an end to the natural, and on the other hand it brings in the spiritual man. That is absolutely essential to God's end. God can never reach His end of conforming us to the image of His Son on natural grounds, in a natural man. If you and I come down on to that carnal level of life, so that we are thinking, feeling, speaking, desiring, choosing and acting upon a natural basis, God can get nowhere with us. That has all to be brought to an end. We are to be fashioned after the Spirit and the spiritual, and then God's end lies full in view, conformity to the image of His Son.

The Cross, the Divide Between Two Creations

Now we pass to the second letter to the Corinthians, and we find our passage in chapter 5 verses 14-18. This is but an advance upon the position in the first letter. There we have seen that the cross brings in the spiritual man in the place of the natural man. The same thing is said here, but the matter is carried further, and enlarged. Its scope is now that of a whole creation. What is clearly before us here is this, that the individual believer through the cross of the Lord

Jesus is constituted a new creation, a member of a spiritual creation, and that everything in this creation in a related way is spiritual; that is, there is a new race, and the natural relationships of all members of that new race are lifted up into the Spirit. The distinction is drawn between that which is after the flesh, and that which is after the Spirit; between anything that is according to the old creation and anything that is according to the new creation; and the cross stands between. "All died", says the apostle; but he says here that all died in Christ in relation to all others. Formerly we knew one another after the flesh, our relationships were carnal relationships, the relationships of an old creation, and we apprized one another according to old creation standards, we judged one another on an old creation basis, our relationships with one another were all along that level of nature, the old creation. Therefore, seeing we have all died in Christ, and have risen, on the new basis we no longer know one another after the flesh, but our relationships are brought into the Spirit; that is, we have been lifted into a new creation realm, into another creation and our fellowship has as its basis the fact that there is a new creation life in us. The fellowship of God's people would not exist five minutes if we were to drop on to the level of nature. It would be in fragments. What is it that holds the people of God together and makes up that very blessed fellowship which is one of the strongest testimonies to the victory of the cross of the Lord Jesus? It is the fact that they share one Spirit, a new creation life, where all is of God. The old things are passed away. We have to act on that basis. We have to adjust ourselves to it.

You notice that this second letter very clearly follows on the position of the first letter. In the first letter you have this: "Ye are carnal; and the proof that ye are carnal is this, that one says, I am of Paul! and another says, I am of Apollos! and another says, I am of Peter! When everyone says 'I', which proves ye are carnal". Is not that the very hallmark of the old creation? All our relationships in the old creation do secretly seem to be gathered round the "I" interest; just where we figure in the matter; how the thing affects us;

what we are going to gain or lose; our satisfaction. If a person in the old creation does not like us we just wash our hands of them and say, "Well, all right, it does not matter, you can go." That is commonly how it affects us. If, on the other hand, people like us, then we hold these to ourselves. We like to be liked, and we have no interest in that which does not gratify that "I" in some form or another. It is shot through all our social relationships. It is shot through our commercial relationships. It is shot through the whole of the old creation. Somewhere you will find that "I" element which governs.

The apostle says that the cross of the Lord Jesus has brought an end to that and our relationships are on a new basis altogether. No longer are the personal benefits from our relationships our consideration, but we know one another after the Spirit, and minister Christ to one another. You are no longer an object upon which I fasten my attention in order to get some benefit from you; my attention is directed towards you in order that I may be of help to you, may minister to you. You hate me; I love you all the more. You work against me; I will pray for you. That is the line of the new creation. It is a different kind of thing. Henceforth we know no man after the flesh.

I am not saying that we always live up to that level, but I am saying that is God's way of conforming to the image of His Son, and when you and I feel that the attitudes of others against us are tending to provoke us to revenge, we have to bring it to the cross, and say, Calvary forbids that. Whenever there is a provoking of what is of the old creation, we have at once to flee to the cross and see to it that it is dealt with then and there: for Calvary means that one died for all, therefore all died, and henceforth we know no man after the flesh.

The Cross and Two Spheres or Modes of Life

We will close with a word on Galatians. What a lot there is in Galatians on the cross. As we have said, there are four great references to the cross in the letter. Of these one passage is especially familiar to us: "For I through the law died unto the law, that I might live unto God. I have been crucified with Christ; yet I live; and yet no longer I, but Christ liveth in me; and that life which I now live in the flesh I live in faith, the faith which is in the Son of God, who loved me and gave himself up for me". (Gal. 2:19-20). The cross of the Lord Jesus, in which I have been crucified! What is the connection of the cross there? It draws the line of distinction between two kinds of lives. You notice what the apostle is saying here. He is saying, in effect, "When I was under the law my quest was for life. I was reaching out for life. I wanted to live before God. I wanted to know what life in fellowship with God was, and in order to know that life of fellowship with God I pursued the law. I followed its injunctions minutely and carefully, I devoted myself to all its commands and its claims. When the law said again and again, 'Thou shalt not', I sought to conform that I might know; and when the law said repeatedly 'Thou shalt', I did all that I could to see that I followed the law. But in my devotion to the law, as that law loomed before me and set such a standard, I discovered that the life in me was contrary to that law. The kind of life that was in me could not correspond with that law, but was always working to the contrary, so that the law became a burden I could not bear, something which ground me down. Instead of saving me, it only made me feel how bad I was. Instead of bringing into life, it only made death a greater reality, because of the life that was in me. I had not the life in me that could reach to the end for which I was seeking, and stand up to God's requirements. The law awoke and I died. How was I to be saved? I shall only be saved if there is another life put into me. If another life is put in me then I shall not need to be told, 'Thou shalt', and, 'Thou shalt not'. I shall have another standard altogether. If only I could have God's life then I should have God's nature, and no one need tell me, "Thou shalt", and, "Thou shalt not", and keep plying me with commandments. I should find that I had in me that which was of God Himself, another life, making everything possible". So the apostle saw the meaning of the cross. "The cross of Jesus Christ", he says, "meant the end of me in that old life, the end of that old very devoted life, that old life that could never get anywhere, that old life that could never stand up to God's requirements. I was crucified with Christ to that life, and therefore, when that life died I died to that realm of things, to that law. Over a dead man no law can operate. Thus through death I escaped the law. But now I live, and yet not I but Christ lives in me; a new life, divine life, Christ Himself lives in me. That is what the cross of Christ has done for me. I had a life which was entirely and utterly incapable of bringing me to any position of rest and satisfaction. It was a life which was no life at all. It was a living death, and I was kept conscious of the fact by the very presence of the law of God. Now, I died with Christ to that life, and died to that law, and I have been raised with Christ, and it is Christ that lives in me now, and by the indwelling life of Jesus Christ I have come to know what Christ is".

It is life upon which the apostle is placing the emphasis here. "That life which I now live in the flesh (*THAT* life) I live in faith, the faith which is in the Son of God who loved me and gave himself up for me". Blessed be God, that is the way of deliverance, the way of emancipation, the way of victory.

We must mention the other three references without dwelling upon them very much. Galatians 3:13-14 so much corresponds to what we have just said, that it would be almost like a reiteration. It is part of the same argument. "Christ redeemed us from the curse of the law, having become a curse for us: for it is written, Cursed is every one that hangeth on a tree: that upon the Gentiles might come the blessing of Abraham in Christ Jesus; that we might receive the promise of the Spirit through faith". Here you have through the cross of the Lord Jesus not only a new life but a new power, and that power is nothing other than the personal presence of the Holy Spirit in the life. We spent much time on that in our last meditation, and need say no more about it, but simply that if the Holy Spirit, God the Holy Ghost, is resident within us on the basis of our resurrection-union with Christ, on the basis of what the death of Christ meant, then all God's purpose is made wonderfully, livingly possible. The Holy Spirit resident within will surely be the power by which we shall come to God's end. This quite naturally works out to the next point in chapter 5 verse 24. "And they that are of Christ Jesus have crucified the flesh with the passions and the lusts thereof".

Here is the cross again, and in this connection it tells us that those who have been crucified with Christ, those who have come into that union with Him in His death and His burial and His resurrection, have a new disposition, "have crucified the flesh with the passions and lusts thereof". They have a disposition against all such things, and have things which are according to Christ. It is a new disposition, or, if you like, a new nature.

Finally, in chapter 6 verse 14: "But far be it from me to glory, save in the cross of our Lord Jesus Christ, through which the world hath been crucified unto me, and I unto the world".

It is interesting to notice the particular way in which the apostle speaks of the world here. That term is a very comprehensive term, and includes a very great deal. Here Paul gets right down to the spirit of the thing. You notice the context. It is well for us to take account of it. "For not even they who receive circumcision do themselves keep the law; but they desire to have you circumcised, that they may glory in your flesh" (verse 13).

What does the apostle mean? They want to say, See how many proselytes we are making! See how many followers and disciples we are getting! See how successful our movement is! See what a power we are becoming in the world! See all the marks of divine blessing resting upon us! The apostle says, That is worldliness in principle and spirit; that is the world. He sets over against this his own clear spiritual position. Do I seek glory of men? Do I seek to be well-pleasing to men? No! The world is crucified to me and I to the world. All that sort of thing does not weigh with me. What weighs with me is not whether my movement is successful, whether I am getting a lot of followers, whether there are all the manifestations outwardly of success; what weighs with me is the measure of Christ in those with whom I have to do. It is wonderful how this at the end of the letter comes right back upon these Galatians, and the whole object of the letter. We recall the words in which that object is summed up. "My little children, for whom I am again in travail, until Christ be formed in you".

Christ formed in you, that is my concern, he says, that is what weighs with me, not extensiveness, not bigness, not popularity, not keeping in with the world so that it is said that this is a successful ministry, and a successful movement. That is worldliness. I am dead to all that. I am crucified with Christ to all that. The thing that matters is Christ, the measure of Christ in you.

You see how the world can creep in, and how worldly we can become almost imperceptibly by taking account of things outwardly; of how men will think and talk, what they will say, the attitude they will take, of the measure of our popularity, the talk of our success. That is all the world, says the apostle, the spirit of the world, that is how the world talks. Those are values in the eyes of the world, but not in the eyes of the risen Christ. In the new creation, on the resurrection side of the cross, one thing alone determines value, and that is, the measure of Christ in everything. Nothing else is of value at all, however big the thing may be, however popular it may be, however men may talk favourably of it; on the resurrection side that does not count a little bit. What counts is how much of Christ there is.

You and I in the cross of the Lord Jesus must come to the place where we are crucified to all those other elements. Ah, you may be unpopular, and the work be very small; there may be no applause, and the world may despise, but in it all there may be something which is of Christ, and that is the thing upon which our hearts must be set. The Lord give us grace for that crucifixion. There are few things more difficult to bear than being despised; but He was despised and rejected of men. What a thing is in God's sight must be our standard. That is a resurrection standard. Now that is the victory of the cross. "God forbid that I should glory, save in the cross of our Lord Jesus Christ..."

So you see that at every point the cross is related to God's full end, conformity to the image of His Son. The Holy Spirit must maintain the cross in operation in us, and we must maintain our attitude and relationship with the cross, to keep the way open and clear for God's end, the image of His Son.

Made in the USA
Coppell, TX
24 June 2021